Indian Cookery

Indian Cookery

Hilary Newstead

WHSMITH

EXCLUSIVE
· BOOKS ·

This edition produced exclusively for
W.H. Smith & Son Limited
Greenbridge Industrial Estate
Greenbridge Road
Swindon
Wiltshire SN3 3LD

Produced by
Bison Books Ltd
176 Old Brompton Road
London SW5 0BA

ISBN 0-86124-382-X

Printed in Hong Kong

The publisher would like to thank the
following for providing some of the props used
in the photographs

David Mellor
4 Sloane Square
London SW1 8EE

David Mellor
26 James Street
Covent Garden
London WC2E 8PA

David Mellor
66 King Street
Manchester M2 4NP

The London Architectural Salvage & Supply
Co Ltd
Mark Street
London EC2A 4ER

McQueen's Florists and Interior Landscaping
13 Pennybank Chambers,
Great Eastern Street
London EC2A 3ET

Adams Antiques
Houghton Road
St Ives
Huntingdon
Cambridge PE17 4RG

Designer: David Copsey
Photographer: Clint Brown
Editor: Jane Laslett
Stylist: Andrea Brown
Home Economist: Hilary Newstead

CONTENTS

Introduction

The diversity of Indian cuisine reflects the varied cultures and influences embodied in this vast country. Regional cooking relies heavily on local produce, so we find coconut playing a major role in South Indian cooking, extensive use of fish and seafood along the Coromandel and Malabar coastlines, wheat and barley relied upon as staples in the northern interior and the famous rice crops supporting the southern and eastern populations.

The unifying factor throughout the country is the use of spices. Some of these are native to India and others have been introduced. This does not automatically mean that all Indian food is 'hot'. Essentially it is only the chillies, cayenne and peppercorns that add fire to a dish and they are by no means obligatory. Of the many spices grown, about 30 are used in everyday Indian cooking. In different combinations and with subtle blending they produce an infinite range of flavours. Originally spices were prized for their medicinal and preserving qualities as well as their ability to enhance ingredients.

Indian cooking has evolved slowly and there is no reason why you should not adapt recipes to suit your own particular taste. The Indians themselves have adopted ingredients and cooking styles from invading powers and trade contacts. The Mogul influence in the sixteenth century brought links with Persian cooks; their lavish use of fruit, nuts and sweetmeat is now firmly embedded in North Indian regional cuisine.

Perhaps the existence of the extended family has helped to keep cooking as an important part of Indian life. Aunts, sisters and grandmothers all live under one roof so cooking is usually a joint effort and traditional methods are still used. These may be laborious, but culinary skill is a matter of great pride to the Indian cook and there is a certain pleasure and satisfaction to be had from these rituals. Most recipes are still handed down from mother to daughter rather than learnt from recipe books and

Curried Beef and Capsicum (page 41) and Pullau Rice (page 66).

weights and measures are rarely used, the cooks relying instead on their instinct and experience. Mealtimes are a family affair and the food is generally discussed and savoured.

However, the time-consuming methods of grinding ingredients on heavy stones is incompatible with the pace of Western life. We're in luck. Liquidizers, food processors, even coffee grinders can all be applied to Indian cookery to enable us to produce delicious food in a fraction of the time. No special equipment need be bought to re-create most dishes but for the perfectionist, Indian shops do sell some of the traditional implements. For deep-frying, Indians use a thick, round-bottomed pan called a kadhai. These are usually made of iron, with handles on both sides rather like a heavy wok. Because they are wide and shallow more items can be cooked in one go. Ordinary deep frying pans are perfectly adequate, as are electric pans as long as they have a variable heat control. Kadhais are also used in making sweets where the milk has to be simmered slowly, as the shape and thickness of the pan prevents burning. Indian breads like chappaties are rolled out on a chakla – a small round board raised on three stumpy legs – using a slim wooden rolling pin which tapers at either end. Again these can be replaced with a pastry board and standard rolling pin. If you make chappaties or parathas often you may find a tawa useful. It is a smooth cast-iron plate, usually with a long wooden handle. The surface is slightly concave and there is no rim around the edge. This also makes an ideal surface on which to fry delicate patties and croquettes as you can slide the food on and off the tawa without

fear of mishap. Where a recipe calls for yoghurt or liquid to be poured through muslin, hung up and left to drip, I make use of a nylon jelly bag which is equally effective and a lot less messy.

Shopping or marketing in India is a colourful and noisy business. Most items of food are bought fresh from local markets. First of all the potential customer inspects the goods carefully while the vendor calls out a price to him. The shrewd customer looks horrified or disgusted, turns away and begins to scrutinize rival goods. Invariably the customer returns to the first stall and buys the same goods but at a much better price. Here, we can buy a huge variety of fruit and vegetables imported from all over the world all year round.

For the growing number of vegetarians in the West, Indian cookery can provide an excellent base, combining the necessary components of a balanced diet with interesting textures and flavours. South India has a vast vegetarian population, some for moral and religious reasons, others through necessity. The meatless cuisine of this region is tasty and extremely varied and includes pulses, vegetables, grains and some dairy products, notably thick plain yoghurt.

To serve an Indian meal you should prepare an interesting selection of dishes – meat and/or fish, one or two vegetable recipes, rice and perhaps a dhal, chappaties or puris, pickles, chutney and a simple vegetable sambal. Many of these dishes can be prepared or even cooked the day before. It is important to balance the textures, flavours and consistencies of the food. One or two dishes might be very spicy, in which case they should be countered with a milder recipe and a soothing yoghurt raita. Try to include a crunchy vegetable or crisp-fried bhajis if the main dish is a wet curry and so on.

The food can all be placed on the table at once so that everybody can help themselves or, as often happens in India, you can prepare individual thalis for your guests. A thali is a large flat metal dish into which small bowls or katoris are arranged. Each katori should hold a portion of the selected dishes. Breads such as chappaties, nan or puris are usually served with the thali then, as guests finish them, the rice is brought out and a helping placed in the middle of the thali. It is definitely best to eat this sort of meal with your fingers; dip pieces of the bread into each katori, or pour wet curries over the rice, daintily mix with the fingertips then scoop juicy morsels into your mouth. Initially this seems rather tricky and a little messy. A tip is to keep the fingers tightly together (right hand only) and shape the food into mouth-sized balls, scoop them up to your mouth and use your thumb as a 'pusher' to pop the food into your mouth. After a bit of practice it will feel natural and even enjoyable. Beginners may find food working its way up the hand but etiquette demands that you use only the ends of the fingers. Finger bowls – rose scented perhaps – and decent-sized napkins are essential for this style of eating.

After the main course offer bowls of fresh fruit – apples, pears, oranges, grapes and cherries or prepared fruit such as slices of papaya, mango or pineapple to refresh and cleanse the palate. Alternatively choose a dessert or sweetmeat recipe or tempt your diners with some kulfi, Indian ice cream. An unauthentic but generally welcome accompaniment to your meal might be a bottle of crisp white wine or chilled lager. Draw your meal to a close with a dish of dry-roasted aniseed, fennel and cardamom seeds. A few of these, chewed, help to restore fresh breath and make a perfect ending to your dinner party. Indian shops sell packets of prepared seeds and also scented mixtures called supari. The base of these is perfumed crushed betel nut mixed with other digestives. They are an acquired taste.

Sample Menus

Quick Menus

Chicken and Egg Creamed
Plain Rice
Poppadums
Dry Spiced Chickpeas
Green Chutney
Fresh Fruit

East Coast Fish Curry
Ginger Prawns
Lemon Rice
Poppadums
Khumbar Mattar
Sliced Mango and Papaya

Fried Lamb with Fenugreek
Chunna Dhal with toasted Coconut
Plain Rice
Courgettes and Tomato Curry
Banana Fritters

Keema
Cumin Grated Carrots
Alu Bara Mirchi
Plain Rice
Celery and Walnut Raita
Poppadums

For 4 people

Curried Beef and Capsicum
Tandoori Chicken
Paneer Mattar
Nan
Aubergine Sambal
Fresh Fruit

Maharashtran Chicken
Pullau Rice
Cumin Grated Carrots
Toovar Dhal and Egg
Poppadums
Lemon and Lime Pickle
Shrikhand

Roghan Josh
Chicken Korma
Exotic Spiced Rice
Chappaties
Brinjal Boortha
Dry Spiced Chickpeas
Carrot Halva

Spit Roasted Game Birds
Chicken Tikka
Lemon Rice
Parathas
Chickpeas with Toasted Coconut
Celery and Walnut Raita
Simple Courgette Curry
Fresh Fruit

Fried Lamb with Fenugreek
Prawn Kofta
Plain Rice
Spiced Cauliflower
Alu Sukke
Green Chutney
Poppadums
Banana Fritters

Spicy Chicken and Egg
Tandoori Fish
Plain Rice
Puris
Mixed Dhal and Sesame Seeds
Spicy Mango Chutney
Bombay Duck
Kheer

Clockwise from left: Poppadums (page 72), Sliced Papaya and Mango, Lemon Rice (page 67), East Coast Fish (page 33), Khumbar Mattar (page 49), Ginger Prawns (page 28), Spicy Mango Chutney (page 68).

For 6-8 people

Chicken Tikka Kebabs
Green Chutney
Mild Pork
Chicken Biriani
Ginger Prawns
Lemon Rice
Plain Rice
Tomato and Onion Sambal
Cucumber and Capsicum Raita
Selection of Pickles and Chutneys
Poppadums
Mango Fool

Mulligatawny Soup
Keema Stuffed Parathas
Sticky Duck with Pineapple
Pheasant and Apricot Pullau
Beef Vindaloo
Plain Rice
Simple Courgette Curry
Vegetable Dhal
Poppadums
Selection of accompaniments
Sweet Vermicelli and Fresh Fruit

Paneer Pakoras
Green Chutney
Maharashtran Mutton
Cashew-Stuffed Trout
Prawn Bhajis
Stuffed Okra
Pullau Rice (double recipe)
Cumin Grated Carrots
Poppadums
Selection of accompaniments
Quick Kulfi and Fresh Fruit

Vegetarian meals for 2-4 people

South Indian Brinjal Curry
Paneer Mattar
Green Dhal Tarka
Pullau Rice
Poppadums
Lemon and Lime Pickle
Carrot Halva

Vegetable Layer Bake
Spiced Cauliflower
Kitcherie
Puris
Selection of accompaniments
Fresh Fruit

Brinjal Cutlets
Vegetable Samosas
Green Chutney
Vegetable Dhal
Plain Rice
Banana Raita
Kheer

Paneer Pakoras
Green Chutney
Mushroom-Stuffed Cabbage Leaves
Carrot Foogath
Chappaties
Mixed Dhal with Sesame Seeds
Selection of Sambals and Pickles
Fresh Fruit

Vegetarian meals for 6-8 people

Masala Dosai
Green Chutney/Coconut Chutney
Stuffed Okra
Madras Mixed Vegetable Curry
Green Dhal Tarka
Yam Koftas
Plain Rice
Exotic Spiced Rice
Nan
Selection of accompaniments
Rasgullas

Vadais
Coriander Chutney
Alu Bara Mirchi
Brinjal Cutlets
Bhindi Bhaji
Pullau Rice
Toovar Dhal with Egg
Chickpeas with Toasted Coconut
Chappaties
Selection of Sambals and Pickles
Sambar
Almond and Pistachio Burfi

Spices

Asafoetida (Hing)

Asafoetida means 'fetid gum' and is the resin from a plant native to Central Asia. It is sold in Indian shops either as a lump or powdered. The resin lump is hard and dark brown and to use, small pieces have to be chipped off. The powdered form is called compounded asafoetida and is usually mixed with wheat and rice flour and gum arabic. It is used sparingly, mostly in vegetable dishes. There is no close substitute so if you cannot find it, simply omit it from the recipe.

Cardamom (Elaichi)

The small dark seeds are contained in pale green pods. The pods can be used whole or cracked but are not eaten. Alternatively the seeds can be taken out of the pods and used whole or crushed; these are edible. Cardamom has a fragrant aroma and gives food a lemony flavour popular in many Indian desserts. There is also a variety of large, brown cardamom pods which are usually cooked whole, then discarded. These are used in many North Indian rice dishes.

Cayenne Pepper

This hot, red powder is made from dried, ground saataki pepper, which is a type of red chilli. Use it very carefully and reduce the amount stated if you do not care for hot food.

Chillies

Like their cousins the sweet capsicum peppers, chillies vary from green through to red and yellow as they ripen. Chillies grown in Asia have thin pods about 5 cm (2 in) long and impart a fierce spiciness to food. The fatter green chillies from Kenya have a milder flavour, especially if the white seeds are removed before cooking. Dried red chillies are the hottest and if used whole in dishes should be removed before serving. Take great care when slicing and preparing chillies as the cut surfaces can irritate the skin and eyes. If you are wary, wear rubber gloves while handling them. Carefully wash implements after use.

Cinnamon (Dalchini)

Cinnamon sticks are the dried quills of bark from the cultivated cinnamon bush. The sticks are used whole in many rice and meat dishes as a flavouring but are not removed before serving.

Cloves (Lavang)

When the unopened flower buds of the tropical clove tree turn red, they are picked and dried to provide the familiar nail-shaped spice. Used whole the clove is so hard as to be indigestible. Ground cloves form an important part of garam masala, with their distinctive aroma and strong flavour.

Coriander (Dhania)

Both the leaves and seeds of the coriander plant are popular in Indian cookery. The soft green leaves resemble flat Chinese parsley in appearance, but release a remarkable perfume when chopped, bruised or cooked. They are often used to garnish dishes. The light brown round seeds give a very different flavour and are either fried whole or ground to a powder. The seeds are also suitable for dry roasting (see page 11).

Cumin (Zeera)

The seeds of this small herb appear frequently in Indian cookery, often in conjunction with coriander seeds. The cumin seeds most easily available are beige-brown in colour and can be cooked whole but are more commonly ground to a powder. A more expensive variety is the black cumin seed which is smaller and has a slightly different flavour. Cumin can be dry roasted (see page 11) to produce a richer taste.

Fennel

Whole fennel seeds are similar to aniseed in appearance and also have a mild liquorice flavour. Grilled or dry roasted fennel seeds can be chewed to freshen breath.

Fenugreek (Methi)

Generally cooked whole, fenugreek seeds are sandy yellow and oblong shaped. Care must be taken when frying them as they tend to burn easily. Use sparingly.

Ghee (Clarified butter)

Although ghee is considered to be one of the best frying media, it is also one of the most expensive so in most Indian homes oil is used for everyday fare and ghee saved for special dishes. To make ghee, gently melt good quality butter in a narrow heavy pan, then stand the pan in a container of hot water for 30 minutes to settle. Carefully strain off the clear fat, leaving the solid sediment in the pan. Pass the ghee through muslin to remove any scum and refrigerate until needed.

Ginger (Adrak)

Dried ground ginger has been used in European cookery for a long time, but it cannot compare with the fragrant, fresh root ginger which is now commonly available. The root or rhizome is knobbly and should be soft enough to squeeze slightly. Peel and grate, finely chop or grind to a paste with a little water.

Mace (Javitri) Nutmeg (Jaiphal)

These two spices are produced from the same tree. The brown oval seed (nutmeg) grows inside a fibrous lacy husk (mace) which is itself enclosed in the fleshy fruit. Fresh mace is bright red but turns a yellowish brown when dried and it is in this form that we know it best. Both spices can be bought whole or powdered. Whole nutmegs should be finely grated before use but a piece or blade of mace can be added whole to dishes as long as it is fished out before serving.

Mustard Seeds (Rai)

The reddish brown mustard seed is more traditional in Indian cookery, but the more easily obtainable, larger yellow variety may be substituted. They impart 'heat' to food and are usually cooked in hot oil first until they burst or pop to release their full flavour.

Poppy Seeds (Khuskhus)

Like sesame seeds, poppy seeds give a light, nutty flavour to dishes. The tiny seeds are either black or white, the latter being more traditional in Indian cookery.

Pomegranate Seeds (Anardana)

Although not strictly a spice, the dried red seeds of the pomegranate are used as an aromatic. They are only found in specialist Indian food shops, but dried mango powder or grated lemon and orange rind may be used instead.

Saffron (Zafran)

Saffron is obtained from the *Crocus sativus* which is an exotic member of the iris family. The expensive golden saffron threads consist only of the dried styles; these have to be collected by hand. Dry roast the threads over a medium heat then crumble them into hot water or milk. This draws the colour and flavour out of the saffron and the liquid can then be used in cooking. Powdered saffron is also available.

Sesame Seeds (Til)

These can be ground to a powder or used whole to add a nutty flavour. Gingelly oil, made from the pressed seeds, is popular in India for frying and pickling.

Tamarind (Imali)

This tall tropical tree has brilliant clusters of purple and orange flowers which produce brown seed pods about 10 cm (4 in) long. The juicy pulp from the tamarind pods is pressed and sold in slabs like nougat. The rather acid flavour is best extracted by soaking a lump of pressed tamarind in hot water for about 10 minutes. Stir well and pour through a sieve, reserving the liquid and discarding any hard bits. Indian stores also sell pots of smooth dark tamarind paste which is quick and easy to use.

Turmeric (Haldi)

Like ginger, the part of the turmeric plant used in cookery is the rhizome. Fresh root turmeric is difficult to obtain outside Asia, and even there it is usually bought ready dried and powdered. As well as being a digestive, turmeric is the spice that turns dull dishes a glorious yellow. Beware – it will turn many other things yellow too, so avoid spills.

Curry Powder

Curry powders as we know them are not used in India although cooks will sometimes grind special mixes of spices for use in certain dishes. What Indians find abhorrent about commercial powders is that the same blend of seasonings is often used for every dish. There is however no reason why you should not mix and grind your own special blends for you to use as you like. Small quantities are best as ground spices quickly lose their flavour. Here are two recipes for you to try.

General use curry powder

3 tablespoons coriander seeds
1 tablespoon cumin seeds
1 dessertspoon turmeric
2-3 dried red peppers or 1 teaspoon chilli powder
½ teaspoon salt
1 teaspoon cardamom seeds

Heat a heavy-based pan over a medium heat and when hot add the seeds. Dry roast them, shaking the pan occasionally until they begin to turn a shade darker and give off an aroma. Take care not to burn them. Let the seeds cool slightly then add them to the other ingredients and grind to a powder using a pestle and mortar or a coffee grinder. Store in an airtight jar out of direct sunlight.

Sweet curry powder for use with fish and vegetables

3 tablespoons coriander seeds
2 teaspoons cumin seeds
2 teaspoons turmeric
1 teaspoon fenugreek seeds
2 teaspoons cardamom seeds
1 teaspoon ground ginger
1 teaspoon demerara sugar

Heat a heavy-based pan over a medium heat. When hot add the seeds. Shake the pan over the heat until they begin to turn brown. Take particular care not to burn the fenugreek seeds. Cool and mix with the other spices, sugar and salt. Grind to a fine powder in a pestle and mortar or a coffee grinder.

Garam Masala

This is a combination of ground mixed spices. The spices most commonly used are those strong, 'heat-generating' ones such as cinnamon, cloves and peppercorns. Good mixes are sold commercially but not only is it cheaper to make your own but you can also create a blend to suit your individual taste. An electric coffee grinder makes life easier but it is perfectly possible to grind the spices by hand using a rough stone pestle and mortar. To ensure the freshness of your Garam Masala it is advisable to prepare small quantities at a time and store in an airtight jar away from direct sunlight.

Generally the cumin, coriander and cardamom content tones down the strength of the mix so increase the amount used for a milder flavour.

Basic garam masala

1 small stick of cinnamon
1 teaspoon black peppercorns
4 whole cloves

Grind these spices together to a fine powder. This mix is stronger than commercial blends and should be used sparingly.

Special garam masala

1 small stick cinnamon
1 teaspoon black peppercorns
4 whole cloves
½ teaspoon grated nutmeg
1 tablespoon cardamom seeds
2 teaspoons cumin seeds
1 small dried bay leaf
¼ teaspoon mace
2 teaspoons coriander seeds

Grind all the spices together to a fine powder. The blend of spices complement each other well to give a full-flavoured, medium-strength mix.

DRY ROASTING SEEDS

This method of preparing seeds produces a richer, stronger flavour. Place a heavy-based pan over a medium heat and let it get hot. Add the seeds and, shaking the pan every now and then, roast until they turn a slightly darker colour and give off an aroma. Seeds such as mustard tend to explode when they get hot, so have the lid to the pan handy ready to cover it if need be. The roasting should only take a couple of minutes. Cool the seeds slightly then grind them to a fine powder using a pestle and mortar or a coffee grinder. The powder is then ready for use.

Appetizers

Samosas have become popular here and can be bought in supermarkets to take home to augment an Indian meal or simply to be munched as a snack. In India a wide range of this type of cooked savoury is sold on street corners or in cafes.

Many of these are bought early in the morning and taken home for breakfast in a tiffin carrier – a set of stainless steel dishes which sit on top of one another in a metal frame – or are simply wrapped in banana leaves and tied up with cotton.

Some people may find the idea of a spiced breakfast rather daunting and most of these dishes certainly take longer to prepare than a quick slice of toast and a fried egg. However, these snacks are very acceptable at any time of the day.

They can be used to add another course to an Indian meal and vadais, samosas, pakoras and Bombay mix all make interesting nibbles for parties.

Mulligatawny Soup

Soups as we know them are rarely eaten in India. This famous one, much favoured by the British colonialists, is based on a Tamil recipe. A fairly hearty soup, it can be a meal in itself.

450g (1 lb) lean mutton
100g (4 oz) lentils
small piece of pressed tamarind
1 litre (2 pts) good chicken stock
2 onions, chopped
2 green chillies, chopped
2 teaspoons crushed garlic
1 teaspoon grated ginger
4-6 tablespoons oil
2 teaspoons ground cumin
2 teaspoons ground coriander
pinch of grated nutmeg
1 teaspoon turmeric
salt and freshly ground black pepper to taste
50g (2 oz) cooked rice
lemon slices/wedges to garnish

Trim the meat and cut into thin strips. Simmer the lentils and tamarind in ⅓ of the stock for 15 minutes. Rub through a sieve to make a thickened purée and discard any bits of tamarind left behind.

Blend the onion, chillies, garlic and ginger in a liquidizer to make a paste.

Heat the oil in a large frying pan and cook the mutton in batches briskly until it is light brown all over. Remove from the pan and place in a large saucepan. Fry the cumin, coriander, nutmeg and turmeric for a minute or two then stir in the onion paste. Cook over a moderate heat for 5 minutes, stirring all the time. Pour the lentil purée into the pan and mix well. Add this to the meat in the saucepan along with the rest of the stock. Season with salt and pepper and bring to the boil. Lower the heat and simmer gently for about an hour or until the meat is tender. Towards the end of the cooking time stir in the cooked rice and let it warm through.

Serve garnished with lemon slices or wedges.

As a variation try stirring in 25 g (1 oz) of creamed coconut halfway through the simmering time to give a softer, creamy soup.

Uppma

In this recipe semolina is dry roasted before mixing it with the other ingredients to give a light, crumbly texture. The effect is delicious and rather addictive. This recipe comes from South India and can be eaten with your fingers or by using a fork or spoon.

100 g (4 oz) semolina
3 tablespoons oil
1 onion, sliced
2 green chillies, finely chopped
1 dessertspoon grated fresh ginger
1 teaspoon mustard seeds
½ teaspoon turmeric
1 tablespoon dried mango powder (aamchor), optional
1 teaspoon ground cumin
225 g (8oz) grated carrot
50 g (2 oz) peas
450 ml (¾ pint) water
50 g (2 oz) sultanas
50 g (2 oz) flaked almonds
1 tablespoon chopped coriander leaves
salt and pepper to taste
75 g (3 oz) butter

Set a heavy pan over a medium heat and pour in the semolina. Shake and stir the pan occasionally until the semolina turns sandy brown. Remove from the heat.

Heat the oil and fry the onion, chillies, ginger, mustard seeds, turmeric, mango powder and cumin for 3-4 minutes. Stir in the carrots, peas and water. Bring to the boil, lower the heat and simmer gently for 10 minutes with the lid off.

Pour the contents of the pan over the semolina in the frying pan and add the sultanas, nuts and coriander leaves. Carefully work everything together until all the moisture has been absorbed and there are no dry pockets of semolina left. Season with salt and pepper. Cook over a medium heat, stirring gently to maintain the crumbly texture. When the mixture is thoroughly mixed, make a well in the centre and put the butter into it. Let it melt then carefully incorporate this into the uppma. Cook for a further 5 minutes before serving.

Puri Palya

This is probably my favourite breakfast dish in India. It would also make a tasty starter to an Indian meal.

The recipe for puris – puffy, fried bread – is listed with the other breads in the Grains and Pulses Section (see page 60).

Serve one recipe puris with one recipe masala stuffing (see page 14). Allow 3-4 puris per person and serve them with a small dish of palya. Use the puris to scoop up mouthfuls of the potato mixture.

Mulligatawny Soup.

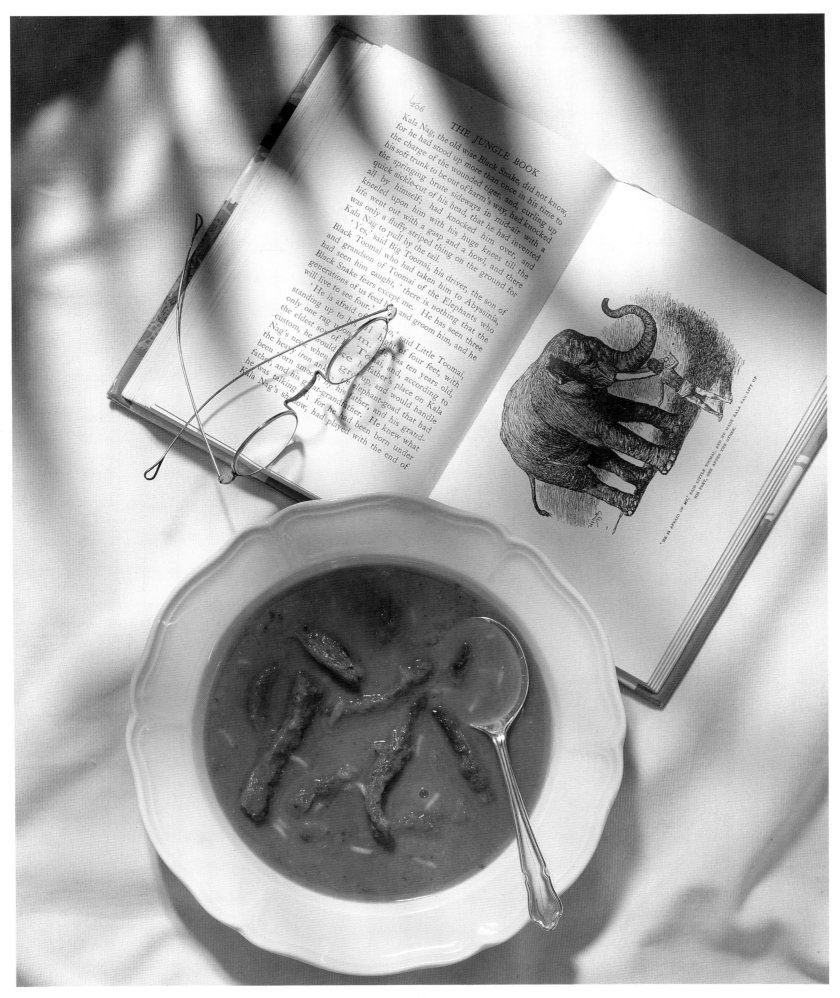

Nargisi Koftas

In this recipe the Nargisi Koftas are deep fried and can be eaten as a snack. They can also be simmered in a sauce until cooked and in this form they make an acceptable main dish. For the sauce, follow the recipe for sambar (see page 16) and stir in 2 tablespoons of plain yoghurt just before serving. Koftas cooked in a sauce will be softer than the fried variety and will take approximately 30-40 minutes to cook.

275 g (10 oz) lean lamb, finely minced
1 teaspoon fresh ginger, grated
2 cloves garlic, crushed
2 fresh green chillies or ½-1 teaspoon chilli powder
1 large onion, finely minced
2 teaspoons garam masala
pinch of ground mace
1 teaspoon ground coriander
½ teaspoon salt
5 eggs, hard-boiled
oil for deep frying

Place all the ingredients except the eggs into a liquidizer or food processor and work them together until you have a smooth-textured paste. Use short bursts of power for this, making sure that the mixture is pushed down to the base of the machine.

Peel the eggs and rinse in cold water. Dry them and, using your hands, coat evenly with the meat mixture. If the meat is rather sticky to work with either wet your hands or dust them with flour.

Heat the oil and deep fry the koftas in batches until they are brown and the meat cooked through.

Paneer Pakoras

Paneer, the Indian version of cottage cheese, is dipped in a spiced batter and fried briefly in oil. The result is surprisingly delicious.

1 litre (2 pints) milk
3 tablespoons lemon juice, warmed
100 g (4 oz) chickpea flour (gram flour)
¼ teaspoon chilli powder
¼ teaspoon salt
½ teaspoon turmeric
½ teaspoon garam masala
300 ml (½ pt) water
oil for deep frying
freshly ground black pepper

Bring the milk to the boil slowly and stir in the warmed lemon juice. When the milk curdles remove from the heat and allow to cool. Pour through muslin or a jelly bag and let all the moisture drip out. Squeeze lightly then place the cheese, still in the muslin or jelly bag, under a weight for at least an hour. You should now have about 175 g (6 oz) of firm paneer. Cut it into bite-sized pieces and leave in the refrigerator while you make the batter.

Sieve the flour, chilli powder, salt, turmeric and garam masala into a bowl. Gradually stir in the water until you have a smooth batter.

Heat the oil in a deep-fat fryer.

Grind plenty of black pepper over the paneer pieces then dip them in the batter. Drop them carefully into the hot oil in batches and cook until they turn crisp and golden brown.

Serve as soon as possible after cooking.

Masala Dosai

These are very popular spicy stuffed pancakes which are often eaten for breakfast. The dosai is the pancake, made from a mixture of ground rice and chickpea flour. In this case masala refers to the spiced potato filling.

Masala Stuffing
1-3 fresh green chillies
1 teaspoon black mustard seeds
1 onion, finely sliced
¼ teaspoon turmeric
½ teaspoon ground cumin
1 teaspoon dried mango powder (aamchor), optional
350 g (12 oz) cooked diced potatoes
salt to taste
4 tablespoons oil
2 tablespoons lemon juice

Slice the chillies finely, discarding the seeds. Heat the oil and fry the mustard seeds until they pop. Keep the lid on during this process. Add all the other ingredients except the lemon juice and stir-fry for 5 minutes. Moisten with the juice and cook for a further 5 minutes. Keep warm until the dosai are ready.

Vadais

Vadais are usually sold in cafes or by street hawkers. This recipe gives golden, puffy Vadais which resemble doughnuts. Accompany with a portion of fresh coriander chutney.

100 g (4 oz) yellow split peas
1 teaspoon bicarbonate of soda
1 onion, chopped
2 cloves garlic, crushed
2 dried red chillies
1 tablespoon coriander leaves, chopped
½ teaspoon salt
1½ tablespoons chickpea flour (gram flour)
oil for deep frying

Soak the split peas in water mixed with ½ teaspoon of bicarbonate of soda for 24 hours. Change the water once during this time. Drain well and allow to dry. Grind the split peas in a liquidizer or food processor until smooth. Add the onion, garlic, chillies, coriander, salt and chickpea flour to the liquidizer. Blend until smooth. Add ¼ teaspoon of the remaining bicarbonate of soda to this mixture.

Heat the oil in a deep frying pan. Take heaped tablespoonfuls of the vadai mix and place on damp muslin. If you cannot obtain muslin, clear fine net curtaining will do. Cover with muslin and pat gently to shape them into flattened balls. Push a finger through the centre to form a ring and carefully transfer to the hot oil, 2 or 3 at a time. The vadais should take 4-5 minutes to cook. If they brown too quickly lower the temperature of the oil as they must be allowed to cook right through. Keep warm until all the vadais are ready.

Instead of the doughnut ring shape, vadais can also be made simply by dropping rounded tablespoonfuls of the mixture into the hot oil.

Eat with your fingers, dipping them into coriander or mint chutney (page 68).

Cocktail Pakoras

These bite-sized nibbles can be passed around as savoury delicacies at drinks parties or simply eaten as a snack. They are best served hot accompanied by a bowl of fresh mint or coriander chutney.

175 g (6 oz) chickpea flour (gram flour)
¼-½ teaspoon chilli powder or cayenne pepper
½ teaspoon salt
1 teaspoon turmeric
½ teaspoon garam masala
1 teaspoon ground coriander
450 ml (¾ pt) water
a selection of cauliflower sprigs, carrot matchsticks, sliced onion,
  capsicum strips, prawns
oil for deep frying

Sieve the flour into a bowl and mix with chilli or cayenne, salt, turmeric, garam masala and coriander. Gradually stir in the water to make a perfectly smooth batter. Allow to stand for 1 hour. Prepare the assorted vegetables. Heat oil in a deep fat fryer until very hot.

Dip the vegetables into the batter and drop them straight into the hot oil, a few at a time. Cook for 1-2 minutes or until golden brown. Drain and place on kitchen paper to absorb any excess oil. Keep cooked pakoras warm in the oven while continuing to fry the remaining pakoras.

Either eat them as they are or dip into a raita – a fresh yoghurt-based chutney (see pages 72-3).

Masala Dosai (right) served with Fresh Coconut Chutney (page 68), thin Toovar Dhal (page 63) and extra stuffing.

Dosai
100 g (4 oz) chickpea flour (gram flour)
25 g (1 oz) ground rice
½ teaspoon salt
pinch of bicarbonate of soda
1 egg
150 ml (¼ pt) milk
60 ml (2 fl oz) water
oil for shallow frying

Sieve the chickpea flour and ground rice into a bowl with the salt and bicarbonate of soda. Beat the egg lightly and mix with the milk and water. Gradually stir this into the bowl to make a smooth batter. Leave for ½ hour before using.

Heat ½ teaspoon of oil in a frying pan and pour in about 2 tablespoons of the batter. Quickly swirl the pan around until the batter covers the base evenly. Cook for 2 minutes on each side or until golden brown. Stack cooked dosai and keep them warm in a low oven until they are all ready.

Spoon some masala stuffing along the middle of each dosai, roll up and the dosai is ready to serve.

Masala dosais are delicious served with either Fresh Coconut Chutney (page 68) or a sambal (page 71).

Samosas

Samosas can be frozen uncooked so it is a good idea to make a large batch at a time, eat some and freeze the rest. Choose either the keema (minced beef) or the vegetable filling or make half and half. They are delicious served with a sambal.

Pastry
175 g (6 oz) plain flour
75 g (3 oz) hard margarine or butter
½ teaspoon salt
1 teaspoon black cumin seeds
few tablespoons of milk
oil for deep frying

Sieve the flour into a bowl. Cut the fat into small pieces and rub into the flour until it resembles breadcrumbs. Mix in the salt and cumin seeds and enough milk to give a soft dough.

Divide into 6 portions and roll these on a pastry board to make smooth balls. Dust the board with flour and roll out into thin rounds. Cut each in half. Have a bowl of water and your prepared stuffing handy. Damp the edges of the pastry semi-circles and form into fat cones. Half fill with the cold stuffing and press the open edges together to seal them. You should end up with triangular patties.

Either freeze the samosas at this stage in sealed bags or deep fry 2 or 3 at a time for 1-2 minutes in moderately hot oil.

Vegetable Stuffing
1-2 fresh green chillies
1 teaspoon ground cumin
1 teaspoon ground coriander
1 teaspoon garam masala
1 teaspoon dried mango powder (aamchor) – optional
40 g (1½ oz) ghee or butter
1 onion, finely chopped
1 teaspoon fresh ginger, grated
200 g (7 oz) cooked potatoes, diced
50 g (2 oz) peas or grated carrots
½ teaspoon dried mint
1 tablespoon coriander leaves, chopped

Finely chop the chillies discarding the seeds. Fry the cumin, coriander, garam masala and mango powder in the ghee or butter for 1 minute then stir in the onion, chillies and ginger. Cook gently until the onion is soft then mix in the potatoes, carrots, mint and coriander. Stir-fry over a low heat for at least 5 minutes, making sure that the vegetables are well coated with the spices. Allow to cool before using.

Keema Stuffing
1 onion, finely chopped
3 tablespoons oil
1 tablespoon chopped coriander
1 teaspoon garam masala
1 teaspoon ground cumin
1 clove garlic, crushed
1-2 fresh green chillies, finely chopped
200 g (7 oz) minced beef
1 tablespoon tomato purée (optional)
½ teaspoon salt

Fry the onion in the oil with the coriander, garam masala, and cumin. Add the garlic and chillies to the pan. When the onion is golden brown, stir in the mince and cook over a moderately high heat until it has browned all over. Stir in the purée if using and water. Cook uncovered over a gentle heat for 20 minutes, stirring occasionally. Season with salt and cook until the mixture is dry. Take care that it does not burn on the bottom of the pan. Leave to cool.

Sambar Sauce

This is the traditional sauce for idlis. It can also play a part in main meals, particularly for vegetarians. Try spooning Sambar over plain rice or serve it with dry dishes. You can vary the amount of lemon juice and tamarind to suit your taste – this recipe gives quite a tangy flavour.

50 g (2 oz) red lentils
1 teaspoon coriander seeds
½ teaspoon mustard seeds
½ teaspoon cumin seeds
3 tablespoons oil
1 onion, sliced
2 cloves garlic, crushed
2 green chillies, chopped with seeds removed
1 teaspoon turmeric
walnut sized piece of pressed tamarind soaked in 300 ml (½ pt) hot water
225 g (8 oz) marrow, peeled and diced (optional)
397 g (14 oz) can tomatoes, pushed through a sieve
1 lemon
½ teaspoon salt
1 tablespoon coriander leaves, chopped, or 1 teaspoon dried fenugreek leaves

If you have the time soak the lentils in cold water for ¾ hour. Heat a heavy-based pan over a medium heat and add the coriander, mustard and cumin seeds. Dry roast until they begin to turn brown. Shake the pan and have a lid handy as the mustard seeds are liable to pop and jump out of the pan. Grind them to a powder using a pestle and mortar or a coffee grinder.

Heat the oil in a saucepan and fry the onion, garlic and chillies with the turmeric, coriander, mustard and cumin for 3 minutes. Pass the tamarind liquid through a sieve, pushing through the pulp and discarding any bits. Pour this into the pan with the marrow, sieved tomatoes, and lentils. Cover and simmer gently until the lentils are soft. Cooking time will vary between 10-20 minutes depending upon whether the lentils were pre-soaked.

Squeeze the juice from the lemon and stir into the sambar with the salt and coriander and fenugreek leaves. The finished consistency should be that of thin soup. To serve with idlis, pour sambar into small individual bowls. Dip the idlis into the sambar briefly so that they absorb the flavour but do not disintegrate, then pop them quickly into your mouth. Extra sambar can be finished up with a spoon.

Idlis

These South Indian steamed rice cakes can either be eaten dipped into fresh coriander chutney or hot sambar. Traditionally Idlis are made from soaked ground rice and pulses, all of which take some time to prepare. The alternative is to use a combination of ground rice or rice flour mixed with urhad dhal flour and water and left to stand overnight. Special idli flour is available from Indian stores and this contains the correct mix of flours.

100 g (4 oz) ground rice and 50 g (2 oz) urhad dhal flour or 175 g (6 oz) idli flour
270 ml (9 fl oz) water
¼ teaspoon bicarbonate of soda
½ teaspoon ground fenugreek
½ teaspoon salt
freshly ground black pepper
15 g (½ oz) butter

Samosas with Keema Stuffing and Fresh Coconut chutney with Coriander (page 68).

Sieve the ground rice with the urhad dhal flour into a basin. If using idli flour sieve it into a basin on its own. Gradually stir in the water until you have a smooth thick batter. Stir in the bicarbonate of soda, cover and leave to stand in a cool place overnight.

Season with the fenugreek and salt and pepper. Grease an egg poacher and set over simmering water.

Spoon the batter into the containers until they are slightly over half full. Cover the pan with a lid and simmer very gently for about 8-10 minutes.

Keep cooked idlis warm in a clean cloth if they are to be eaten with sambar (see page 16). Alternatively, drop the warm idlis into a bowl of fresh coriander chutney (see page 68). Leave them to absorb some of the moisture from the chutney then eat either with a teaspoon or with your fingers.

Bombay Mix

In India this would be called fried channa dhal. There are lots of variations on this theme of crisp fried tit-bits and it is a good way to use up odd small quantities of dried pulses. Extra Bombay Mix can be kept in an airtight jar. Hand round a bowl of Bombay Mix before dinner or at parties.

50 g (2 oz) yellow split peas
50 g (2 oz) assorted dried pulses (not the large types like butter beans, soya beans or chickpeas)
1 teaspoon bicarbonate of soda
oil for deep frying
50 g (2 oz) flaked almonds
50 g (2 oz) unsalted cashew or pistachio nuts
1 teaspoon salt
¼ teaspoon freshly ground black pepper
1 teaspoon garam masala
¼ teaspoon dried mango powder (aamchor), optional
¼-½ teaspoon cayenne pepper

Soak the split peas and pulses in cold water with the bicarbonate of soda overnight. Drain them well and dry by spreading them on a clean cloth or kitchen paper. Heat the oil in a deep fat fryer and add a tablespoon of the soaked pulses at a time. After a couple of minutes they should rise to the surface; cook for a further 2 minutes. Scoop a few out, cool briefly and test them to make sure that they are crisp and not too hard. If all is well remove the cooked pulses using a slotted spoon or metal tea strainer and put them onto kitchen paper. Continue until the rest are cooked.

Deep fry the nuts until they begin to turn brown, and add them to the pulses.

Tip the nuts and pulses onto clean kitchen paper to remove excess oil and sprinkle all the spices and seasonings over. Shake to make sure everything is coated with the flavourings. Bombay Mix is delicious served either warm or cold.

Poultry and Game

Chickens are not cheap to buy in India, nor are they as plump and tender as the ones sold here. But the rather scrawny hens used in so many marvellous Indian dishes are, in fact, extremely tasty.

Generally the skin is removed before marinading or cooking to allow the selected aromatics to fully impregnate the meat. Marinading also tenderizes the flesh, a process which is not as important here. In extreme cases, tough old birds are either wrapped in papaya leaves or smothered in papaya purée before slow cooking.

Usually the meat is left on the bone but if you prefer, boneless breasts may be used instead of jointing whole chickens. One breast per person is an ample serving.

Chicken is very versatile, the soft white meat readily absorbs and complements a whole range of flavours from delicate cardamom and coconut to fiery chillies and the whole spices used in birianis.

As well as the famous Tandoori, Biriani and Korma recipes, which all have their roots in the north of India, some marvellous regional chicken dishes are included. The Maharashtran Chicken recipe uses cashew nuts and coconuts, which are plentiful along the western coastline, to produce a delicious, creamy dish. The Kashmiris, way up in the foothills of the Himalayas, use strong, hot spices in some of their dishes and then in others leave them mild and subtle. The Kashmiri Chicken recipe given here is of the powerful variety, but the chillies which provide most of the 'fire' are optional.

Game birds are as prized in India as in other parts of the world. Pheasant, partridge, green pigeon, snipe, wild duck and quail are all found. In the land where even tea may be flavoured with cardamom seeds, it is not surprising that spices are encouraged to work their magic on these birds too.

Tandoori Chicken

This is one of India's most famous dishes. Tandoori preparations are traditionally marinaded for several hours and then cooked very quickly in the clay tandoor oven, which is heated by charcoal. Juicy lemon wedges are often served with Tandoori Chicken to give it a wonderful tanginess. Try it with plain rice, pickles and tomato pitla.

1 plump chicken, jointed or 4 large chicken pieces
2 lemons
6 cloves of garlic, crushed
250 ml (8 fl oz) thick, plain yoghurt
1 teaspoon garam masala
½ teaspoon paprika
1 teaspoon turmeric
2 teaspoons ground coriander
½ teaspoon salt
1 tablespoon oil
25 g (1 oz) butter
few drops of red food colouring (optional)

Skin the chicken and place in a dish. Pour the juice of 1 lemon over and leave to stand for ½ hour.

Combine with the garlic, yoghurt, spices, salt, oil, softened butter and a few drops of red food colouring.

Cut deep slashes across the chicken flesh and smother with the thick marinade. Leave for at least 12 hours.

Heat the oven to its maximum temperature and grease the bars of the top rack. Place a roasting tin under the rack to catch the drips. When the oven is really hot lay the chicken pieces on the rack and close the door. Leave to cook for 8-10 minutes, basting once or twice with the marinade. Turn the chicken pieces over and repeat for the other side.

The chicken is ready when it starts to blacken at the edges, yet is moist and cooked in the centre.

Cut the remaining lemon into quarters and serve one with each piece of chicken.

Chicken Tikka Kebabs

**These are really tasty morsels of chicken, marinated then skewered and grilled. Usually they are served before the main part of a meal as an appetizer but just increase the amount of meat used and serve with yellow rice and a selection of sambals to make a delicious main meal.
Chicken Tikka Kebabs also make a tasty light supper for slimmers when served with a generous portion of fresh salad.**

750 g (1½ lb) boned chicken breasts
1 lime
2-3 cm (1 in) piece of fresh ginger, grated
1 teaspoon paprika
2 cloves of garlic, crushed
50 g (2 oz) soft butter
1 teaspoon ground coriander
1 teaspoon ground cumin
¼ teaspoon salt
pinch of grated nutmeg
4 tablespoons plain yoghurt
a little oil

Rub the chicken with the cut lime and ginger. Cut the chicken breasts into bite-sized chunks.

Squeeze the rest of the juice from the lime and place in a bowl. Add all the other ingredients to the bowl, except the oil. Mix well to make the marinade and pour over the chicken chunks. Leave for 12 hours.

Brush metal skewers with oil and thread the chicken onto them. Heat the grill and when very hot, slide a tray of the kebabs under. Cook for 15-20 minutes, turning and basting with the marinade every 5 minutes.

They should be a little bit crusty on the outside and moist in the middle when cooked.

Tandoori Chicken.

Duck in Ginger Cream

In this recipe the duck is roasted separately, then added to a wonderfully rich ginger sauce. For the calorie counters among you, replace the cream with yoghurt. It tastes very good served with channa dhal, fried coconut and plain rice.

2 kg (4 lb) duck
1 orange
½ teaspoon salt
1 tablespoon oil
1 large onion, finely chopped
3 tablespoons milk
few strands saffron
1 tablespoon ground coriander
8 fenugreek seeds
1 teaspoon paprika
25 g (1 oz) ground almonds
250 ml (8 fl oz) thick cream
3 nuggets of sweet stem ginger in syrup

Leave the skin on the duck and wipe it inside and out with kitchen paper. Prick the skin with a cocktail stick in about 6 places.

Mix 2 tablespoons of the ginger syrup with the grated rind of the orange, salt and a pinch of the paprika. Rub this into the skin of the duck. Set the oven to Gas Mark 6, 200°C, 380°F and heat a roasting tin with 1 tablespoon of oil in it. When it is hot lay in the duck, breast side down and roast for 1½ hours. Turn the duck over halfway through the cooking time and baste with its own juices every 20 minutes. The duck should be cooked and the skin crisp and brown. Put the duck in another tin and leave it in a warm oven until you are ready for it.

Fry the onion until soft and golden brown in a little of the fat from the duck. Remove and liquidize until very smooth.

Warm the milk and pour onto the saffron. Allow to stand for 15 minutes.

Using a further tablespoon of the duck fat, fry the coriander, fenugreek seeds and the rest of the paprika. Squeeze the juice from the orange and pour onto the spices in the pan. Cook until the pan is almost dry then stir in the onion purée, ground almonds and infused milk. Gradually add the cream, stirring all the time until you have a rich glossy sauce. Chop the stem ginger and add to the pan.

Either divide the duck into four pieces or cut it into small chunks (on the bone) using poultry scissors. Try to keep the skin intact.

Just before you are ready to serve pour the sauce over the duck pieces. If the duck sits in the sauce for too long the skin loses its crispness.

Barbecued Chicken Pieces

These are two simple marinades for chicken which can then be grilled or cooked outdoors over a charcoal fire. For a barbecue party it is nice to use both marinades (separately) and serve guests with some of each as the flavours complement each other. Although not typically Indian, these chicken pieces are good with a rice salad and chutney.

Tomato marinade

1 large onion
2 cloves of garlic
rind of ½ lemon, grated
¼ teaspoon crushed mustard seeds
1 teaspoon paprika
2 tablespoons tomato purée
4 tablespoons oil
2 teaspoons ground coriander
1 teaspoon honey
pinch of salt

Blend all the ingredients together in a liquidizer.

Fragrant pineapple marinade

1 small onion
½ lemon rind, grated
2 teaspoons fresh ginger, grated
25 g (1 oz) soft butter
150 ml (¼ pt) plain yoghurt
1 tablespoon chopped coriander leaves
4 slices pineapple
1 teaspoon ground cumin
1 fresh chilli
6 green cardamom pods, cracked

Blend all the ingredients except the cardamoms in a liquidizer, then stir in the cracked cardamom pods.

Skin and joint 1 chicken. Slash the flesh and cover with the marinade of your choice. Leave for 12 hours.

Grill or barbecue for about 10 minutes on each side or until the chicken is no longer pink inside. Baste frequently with the appropriate marinade.

Maharashtran Chicken and Cashew Nut

This recipe contains coconut and cashew nuts, both of which are plentiful along the western coast of India. The result is a rich, mustard yellow sauce that is irresistible. Serve with plain rice or puris, sweet mango chutney and poppadums.

5 tablespoons oil
2 onions, sliced
3 cloves of garlic, crushed
1 chicken, jointed
1 tablespoon grated fresh ginger
1 teaspoon turmeric
1 teaspoon ground cumin
2 tablespoons chopped fresh coriander leaves
3 dried red chillies, chopped
1 teaspoon garam masala
pinch of all-spice
300 ml (½ pt) buttermilk
pinch of salt
50 g (2 oz) creamed coconut
25 g (1 oz) ghee or butter
4 tablespoons plain yoghurt
100 g (4 oz) unprocessed cashew nuts

Heat the oil in a sauté pan and fry the onion and garlic for 2 minutes. Add the chicken pieces and stir in the ginger, turmeric and ground cumin. Shake the pan over the heat to prevent anything sticking and turn the chicken so that it is sealed all over. Mix together the coriander, chillies, garam masala, all-spice, buttermilk and a pinch of salt.

Pour this into the pan and stir, carefully coating the chicken with the sauce. Heat until it is barely simmering, then add the creamed coconut with the ghee or butter. This will thicken the sauce.

Do not allow the mixture to boil as the buttermilk will curdle. Transfer into an ovenproof dish, cover and cook in the oven at Gas Mark 4, 180°C, 350°F for ½ hour. Stir in the yoghurt and cashew nuts, turn the oven down to Gas Mark 3, 160°C, 330°F and continue to cook for ½ hour.

Garnish with fresh coriander leaves to serve.

Pineapple Barbecued Chicken Pieces (left); Duck in Ginger Cream (right).

Chicken Biriani

The food of northern India, in particular the Punjab, owes much to foreign influence. When the Moguls came to India in the sixteenth century, they brought with them cooks who knew many exotic Persian recipes. The combination of fruit, nuts and meat was adopted by the Indians and now forms the base of many north Indian specialities. Traditionally birianis are prepared for special occasions such as feasts and weddings. They are very rich, highly aromatic dishes which are well worth the extra time to cook them.

1 chicken
2-3 cm (1 in) fresh ginger, peeled
5 cloves of garlic
3 large onions
100 g (4 oz) ghee or butter
150 ml (¼ pt) plain yoghurt
2 teaspoons ground coriander
salt
10 cm (4 in) stick of cinnamon
10 cloves
350-400 g (12-14 oz) basmati rice
6 large black cardamom pods
1 bay leaf
5 black peppercorns
4 tablespoons oil
1½ teaspoons turmeric
¼ teaspoon grated nutmeg
100 g (4 oz) sultanas
100 g (4 oz) almonds or cashew nuts

Skin the chicken and cut into small joints. Slash the flesh with the point of a knife and rub with ginger and garlic.

Next prepare the marinade for the chicken. Chop one of the onions and fry in 25 g (1 oz) of butter until golden but still soft. Remove from the pan with a slotted spoon and place in a liquidizer or food processor. To this add the yoghurt, peeled ginger, 3 cloves of garlic, ground coriander, 25 g (1 oz) ghee or butter and ¼ teaspoon of salt. Blend together at high speed to give a rich paste. Cover the chicken pieces with the marinade and allow to stand for at least 3 hours.

Transfer to a large flameproof casserole, pop in half of the cinnamon stick with 5 cloves and bring to the boil. Cover tightly and cook in a medium oven until the chicken is tender, approximately 1 hour.

Wash the rice and, if possible, allow to stand in cold water for 1 hour. Slice the remaining onions and crush the other 2 cloves of garlic.

Crack open the black cardamoms and combine with the bay leaf, and remaining cinnamon, cloves and peppercorns. Tie them up in a piece of muslin to make a little pouch.

Heat the rest of the ghee or butter and oil in a lidded pan and fry half of the sliced onions with the garlic. Sprinkle in the turmeric and grated nutmeg with the drained rice. Stir over a medium heat for 5 minutes or until the rice becomes translucent.

Pour over boiling water to cover the rice by 3 cm (1½ in). Season with a little salt, stir, then add the aromatic pouch. Cover and cook slowly until the water has been absorbed, yet the rice still has a slight 'bite' to it.

Stir in the sultanas and nuts and remove the pouch.

Taking a tablespoon of the rice at a time, mix it into the cooked chicken, which should still have some of the liquid marinade with it. When it has all been incorporated, cover again and return to the oven for ½ hour.

When ready to serve, fry the rest of the sliced onion until crisp and use this to garnish the biriani.

Spit Roasted Game Birds

This is a general recipe which can be used for most types of game birds. Choose young birds for this method of preparation. The number of birds required depends upon the type of bird chosen and, of course, their size. As a rough guide: 1 pheasant or wild duck will serve 3 or 4 people; 1 partridge will serve 2 people; 1 pigeon, grouse or poussin will serve 1 or 2 people; 1 quail will serve 1 person.

game birds of your choice
1 teaspoon whole cumin seeds
1 teaspoon whole coriander seeds
10 fenugreek seeds
1 teaspoon black mustard seeds
3 cloves garlic
2 tablespoons grated fresh ginger
½-1 teaspoon chilli powder
300 ml (½ pt) thick plain yoghurt
50 g (2 oz) ground almonds
50 g (2 oz) soft butter

Pheasant with Apricot Pullau

The use of apricots in this dish make it rather sweet. If this is not to your taste, any of the other pullau recipes may be substituted.
Choose a plump, young hen pheasant and do not skimp on the marinading time, as the flavours must be allowed to impregnate the bird thoroughly.
This is a complete meal on its own, or may make a centrepiece for a dinner party.

1 tablespoon grated fresh ginger
2 cloves of garlic, crushed
juice of ½ a lemon
6 tablespoons plain yoghurt
pinch of allspice
75 g (3 oz) ghee or butter
1-2 pheasants, cleaned and plucked
2 onions, sliced
4 tablespoons oil
1 red chilli, chopped
1 teaspoon turmeric
2 teaspoons ground cumin
275 g (10 oz) basmati rice
3 cloves
2-3 cm (1 in) stick of cinnamon
1 teaspoon garam masala
½ teaspoon salt
100 g (4 oz) dried apricots
100 g (4 oz) blanched, skinned almonds

To prepare the marinade combine the ginger, garlic, lemon juice, yoghurt and all-spice. Season with salt.

Remove the skin from the pheasant and wipe inside and out with kitchen paper. Cut through the breast bone and open the bird out. Cover it with a piece of greaseproof paper and give it a couple of gentle blows with a rolling pin to persuade the bird to lie flat. Pour the marinade over, making sure it is completely coated, and leave for 12-24 hours.

Heat 50 g (2 oz) ghee or butter in a shallow lidded pan and when it begins to foam, add the pheasant with all the marinade. Cook until dry and the bird is sealed on both sides. Pour in 250 ml (8 fl oz) of boiling water and stir to incorporate any sediment on the bottom of the pan. Cover the pan and simmer very gently until the pheasant is cooked (about 45 minutes), checking occasionally and adding more water if necessary. Allow to sit in the liquid until you are ready for the pheasant.

Wash the rice and drain well. Slice the onions and fry in the remaining ghee or butter and oil. When the onions begin to brown stir in the chilli, turmeric and cumin. Cook for 2 minutes then stir in the rice. Stir over a medium heat for 3 minutes then pour in ½ l (1 pt) of boiling water. Add the cloves, cinnamon, garam masala and ½ teaspoon salt to the pan. Stir well, cover tightly and cook until the liquid has been absorbed and the rice is almost cooked. Fork in the apricots and almonds.

Take half of the pullau rice and place in a large casserole dish. Remove the pheasant from the pan and either cut into joints or take the meat off the carcass and shred it. Put this on top of the rice and pour over the remaining liquid from the pan. Cover over with the rest of the rice mixture.

Cover tightly and cook for 30 minutes at Gas Mark 3, 165°C, 330°F or until the mixture is heated through.

Wipe the birds inside and out with kitchen paper, but do not wash them as this removes some of their flavour. Leave the skin on if preferred, but cut slashes across the breasts and legs.

Heat a heavy-based pan and dry roast the cumin, coriander, fenugreek and mustard seeds until they turn a little darker, but do not allow them to burn. Remove from the pan and grind to a powder with a pestle and mortar or in a coffee grinder.

Crush the garlic and combine it with the powdered seeds, ginger, chilli powder and yoghurt. Pour this marinade over the birds, making sure they are completely coated. Leave for 12 hours.

Thread the birds onto metal skewers or the spit in the oven if you have one. Allow some of the marinade to drip into a bowl and mix this with the ground almonds and soft butter. Sprinkle salt over the birds.

Either cook over an open fire or in a hot oven Gas Mark 7, 220°C, 425°F. If you do not have a spit attachment in your oven, set the skewers over a deep roasting tin so that the birds can be turned without touching the tin.

Cook and turn the birds, basting frequently with the buttery marinade. Allow 15-20 minutes for small birds and up to 45 minutes for a medium-sized duck. The skin should be dry and crusty and the meat juicy but not bloody when ready.

Serve with cumin grated carrots, exotic spiced rice and walnut and cucumber raita.

Spit-Roasted Poussin.

Chicken Mollee (left); Chicken Saag (right).

Kashmiri Chicken

In northern India and Kashmir the 'strong' aromatic spices, which go to make up garam masala, are very important. Often these spices are used whole and are not eaten, for example cinnamon sticks, blade mace and cloves. Certainly whole spices taste fresher than stale ground powders, so do try them. This dish can also be cooked without any chillies at all to give a less fiery sauce. As it stands this recipe is fairly strong and should leave you glowing at the end of your meal. To complement it, serve with nan or lemon rice, beans in akni and some thick creamy yoghurt raita.

4 chicken portions
½ lemon
3 onions
1 cm (½ in) fresh ginger
5 tablespoons oil
2 cloves of garlic, crushed
2-3 cm (1 in) stick of cinnamon
5 cloves
6 whole green cardamom pods
½ teaspoon ground cumin
5 dried red chillies (optional)
8 tomatoes, quartered
2 tablespoons tomato purée
pinch of sugar
pinch of salt

Skin the chicken and rub with the lemon and then with salt. Slice the onions into rings. Peel the ginger and leave whole. Heat the oil in a large pan and fry the onions until golden brown. Stir in the garlic, ginger, cinnamon, cloves, cardamom pods, cumin and chillies. Continue to cook and stir for 2 minutes. Add the tomatoes with the purée, sugar, salt and 300 ml (½ pt) of water. Bring to the boil, and pour over the chicken in an ovenproof dish.

Place in the centre of the oven and cook for 1 hour or until the chicken is tender and the oil has risen to the top. Set the oven to Gas Mark 5, 200°C, 370°F for the first half an hour then turn it down to Gas Mark 3, 170°C, 325°F for the rest of the time.

Skim off the oil from the top. Remove the piece of ginger along with the whole spices before serving.

Chicken Mollee

This recipe comes from the southwestern state of Kerala, where the coconut palms form a thick, dark band of green along the coast. Mollees are poultry, fish or vegetables cooked in thin coconut milk, an infusion of coconut flesh and water. Here, where good fresh coconuts are not easily found, creamed coconut makes an acceptable substitute. Serve with plain rice, crisp Bombay duck and pickles.

24

Chicken Saag

Nothing could be simpler than this two-stage recipe. The spinach is puréed with herbs, spices and ground nuts to give a velvety green sauce in which the chicken is simmered. Slow cooking is recommended to allow the flavour to develop. For a tasty and attractive meal, serve with yellow rice and coconut chutney and a vegetable dish, if liked.

2 onions, chopped
225 g (8 oz) lightly cooked spinach
2 cloves garlic, chopped
1 tablespoon ground cumin
1 teaspoon ground coriander
2-3 fresh green chillies
¼ teaspoon grated nutmeg
1 tablespoon chopped mint leaves
½ tablespoon chopped coriander leaves
50 g (2 oz) ground almonds
pinch of all-spice
salt and black pepper
425 ml (15 fl oz) chicken stock
25 g (1 oz) ghee or butter
1 chicken, skinned and jointed

Press all the moisture out of the cooked spinach. Place all the ingredients except the chicken and ghee or butter in a liquidizer and work to a smooth consistency.

Melt the butter and let it begin to sizzle and foam. Pour in the spinach sauce, stirring to incorporate the butter. Cook for 5 minutes uncovered then lay in the pieces of chicken. Cover and cook as gently as possible until the chicken is tender and cooked through, about 45 minutes. Alternatively, transfer to a casserole and bake in a slow oven Gas Mark 3, 170°C, 325°F for 1½-2 hours.

Creamed Chicken and Egg

This recipe can be used for leftover cooked chicken and is quick and simple to make. Serve it with rice or puris and a spicy vegetable dish.

400 g (14 oz) cooked chicken
50 g (2 oz) ghee or butter
2 tablespoons oil
2 onions, chopped
2 teaspoons homemade or bought curry powder
25 g (1 oz) ground rice or cornflour
300 ml (½ pt) milk or buttermilk
50 g (2 oz) ground almonds
salt and pepper
150 ml (¼ pt) cream
3 hard-boiled eggs, quartered

Cut the chicken into bite-sized pieces.

Heat the ghee or butter and oil in a roomy pan and fry the onions until golden. Stir in the curry powder and cook for 1 minute. Add the ground rice or cornflour and cook gently for a further minute. Gradually stir in the milk or buttermilk and allow to thicken over the heat.

Add the chicken, ground almonds and salt and pepper. Simmer gently for 20 minutes then pour in the cream and the quartered hard-boiled eggs. Cook for 5 more minutes, but do not let the creamy sauce boil and take care not to break up the pieces of egg.

½ teaspoon turmeric
1 carrot, sliced
2 onions
6 black peppercorns
pinch of salt
1 chicken
1 clove of garlic
2-3 cm (1 in) piece of fresh ginger
1 fresh coconut or 25 g (1 oz) creamed coconut
3 tablespoons oil
3 fresh or dried chillies, sliced
1 teaspoon all-spice
4 whole green cardamom pods

In a large pan half filled with water, put the turmeric, carrot, one onion, peppercorns and salt. Bring to the boil and lower in the whole chicken. Simmer gently with the lid on until the chicken is just cooked. Remove from the pan, take the flesh off the bone. Cut it into even chunks.

Roughly chop other onion. Liquidize this with the garlic. If the ginger is tender, peel and thinly slice, otherwise grate it. Add it to the onion and garlic. Grate the coconut flesh and pour ¼l (½ pt) of boiling water over and leave for ½ hour. Strain and reserve the liquid. If using creamed coconut, dissolve in the hot water.

Heat the oil and fry the onion mixture, stirring continuously until all the moisture has evaporated. Add the chillies with the all-spice and cardamoms. Cook for 3 minutes, then stir in the cooked chicken and half of the coconut liquid. Transfer to an ovenproof dish, cover and cook in the oven for ½ hour at Gas Mark 4, 180°C, 350°F.

Use the rest of the coconut milk if the dish appears dry.

Chicken Korma

Kormas were introduced into India by the Moguls four hundred years ago and are still as popular today. There are many variations on the korma theme, but they all use thick yoghurt as the base of a marinade and are generally not very 'hot', relying on a subtle use of spices. Kormas are best served with lemon rice and a selection of sambals and pickles.

1 plump chicken
4 cloves of garlic
1 tablespoon chopped bottled stem ginger or fresh root ginger
¼ teaspoon salt
250 ml (8 fl oz) thick plain yoghurt
2 large onions
25 g (1 oz) ghee or butter
3 tablespoons oil
½ teaspoon turmeric
¼ teaspoon black mustard seeds
1 teaspoon cumin
1 teaspoon ground coriander
¼ teaspoon paprika
25 g (1 oz) creamed coconut

Skin the chicken and cut into small joints. Crush the garlic and mix half of it with the ginger, salt and half of the yoghurt. Pour this over the chicken pieces, making sure that they are thoroughly coated. Leave for 12 hours.

Chop 1 onion finely. Heat the butter and oil in a large shallow pan and fry the onion with the rest of the garlic. Stir in all the spices and cook for 3 minutes. Add the chicken pieces and continue to cook until the chicken is sealed on all sides.

Transfer the chicken into an ovenproof dish. Pour the remaining yoghurt and any extra marinade into the pan and stir in the spicy residue. Add the creamed coconut and stir over a gentle heat until it has melted. If you are using a large chicken, add a little water to the pan then pour the sauce over the chicken, cover and cook slowly for 1½-2 hours.

When nearly ready to serve, slice the other onion and fry until crisp and golden brown. Scatter the onion pieces over the korma and serve immediately.

This dish tastes just as good, if not better, reheated and served the following day.

Chicken Papaya Masala

Puréed papaya or pawpaw is sometimes used as the base of a marinade because it helps to tenderize meat. Chickens available here do not strictly need such treatment, but the flavour given by the papaya is delicious. Serve with plain rice and spinach kofta.

4 chicken breasts
1 large papaya (also known as pawpaw)
1-2 cloves of garlic
1 teaspoon paprika
2 tablespoons chopped coriander leaves
½ teaspoon salt
250 ml (8 fl oz) plain thick yoghurt
1 large onion, sliced
50 g (2 oz) ghee or butter
1 teaspoon sugar
1½ teaspoons garam masala

Skin the chicken breasts and prick all over with a cocktail stick. Place in a bowl. Remove the skin from the papaya with a knife or potato peeler and cut in half lengthways. Scoop out the juicy seeds and discard them. Liquidize one half of the fruit with the garlic, paprika, chopped coriander, salt and half of the yoghurt. Pour this over the chicken and leave for 12 hours.

Slice the onion into rings. Heat the ghee or butter in a shallow pan and add the onion. Take care that the ghee or butter does not burn and cook until the onions are soft and golden. Sprinkle in the sugar and stir until the onions are coated with the sugary butter and begin to darken.

Put the chicken pieces into the pan with all the marinade and cook for 4 minutes on each side. Shake the pan frequently to prevent the marinade burning. Work in the remaining yoghurt with the garam masala and cover the pan. Cook very gently for a further 15 minutes on top of the oven or for 30 minutes in a moderate oven (Gas Mark 4, 180°C, 350°F).

Slice the other half of the papaya and use it to garnish the dish.

Sticky Duck with Pineapple

This is an adaptation of a Maharashtran recipe for a sweet and sour dish. Originally used with vegetables, I have found it to be a very good combination of flavours for duck. Try it with pullau rice or parathas and alu sukke (spiced potatoes). Serve with spicy prawn or lime pickle to complement the sweetness of the duck.

1 plump duck
3 tablespoons thick honey
2 tablespoons grated ginger
2 cloves garlic, crushed
walnut-sized piece of tamarind
4 tablespoons oil
1 teaspoon black mustard seeds
¼-½ teaspoon chilli powder
1 pinch of compounded asafoetida
2 onions, sliced
1 tomato, roughly chopped
1 small pineapple
lemon or lime juice to taste
salt and pepper

Cut the duck into 6-8 pieces, leaving the flesh on the bone. Leave the skin on, but trim away some of the fat where it is thick.

Mix together the honey, ginger, garlic and a pinch of salt. Spread this over the skin of the duck.

Pour 150 ml (5 fl oz) of boiling water onto the tamarind and leave to stand for 10 minutes. Strain through a sieve, pushing the pulpy tamarind through. Reserve the liquid and discard any bits left in the sieve.

Heat the oil in a large shallow pan. When it is hot add the mustard seeds and cook, covered, until they pop. Stir in the chilli powder, asafoetida and onions and fry for 5 minutes. Add the duck pieces and let them cook for a few minutes on each side.

Mix the tamarind water with the tomato and pour it into the pan. Cover and simmer until the duck is tender.

Peel the pineapple and chop half of the flesh very finely.

Remove the lid and cook until all the moisture has evaporated, stirring to prevent burning. When the pan is dry add the pineapple and mix thoroughly. Adjust the seasoning with the lemon or lime juice and ground black pepper. Continue to stir until the duck is coated with the sticky sauce.

Use the remaining half of the pineapple to garnish the dish.

Chicken Dupiaza

This is a mild chicken dish cooked with plenty of onions. In this particular recipe the onions appear in two forms, puréed and fried. Other recipes use onions to flavour stock in which the chicken is poached and then again fried to make a garnish.

1 chicken, jointed
½ lemon
2-3 cm (1 in) piece of fresh ginger
1 clove of garlic
3 large onions
75 g (3 oz) ghee or butter
3 tablespoons oil
6 whole green cardamom pods
1 teaspoon cumin
1½ teaspoons coriander
2 cloves
½ teaspoon garam masala
½ teaspoon salt
175 ml (6 fl oz) plain yoghurt

Skin the chicken joints and rub with the lemon and the cut edge of the fresh ginger.

Grate the ginger, crush the garlic and chop 2 of the onions.

Heat half of the ghee or butter with the oil in a frying pan and sweat the ginger, garlic and onions over a low heat with the lid on. When they are soft and just starting to turn pale golden remove from the pan with a slotted spoon and liquidize to a smooth purée.

Add the remaining ghee or butter to the pan and stir in the cardamoms, cumin, coriander and cloves. Fry for one minute then lay in the chicken pieces. Cook for 3 minutes on each side then place them in an ovenproof dish.

Pour the puréed onion mixture into the pan and stir well to incorporate the fried spices. Sprinkle in the garam masala and salt and gradually work in the yoghurt. Stir over a gentle heat until the sauce begins to bubble around the edge of the pan. Pour this over the chicken, cover and bake for 45 minutes at Gas Mark 4, 180°C, or 350°F.

Meanwhile slice the remaining onion and fry until crisp and golden brown. Scatter over the top of the chicken 10 minutes before the end of the cooking time.

Sticky Duck with Pineapple.

27

Fish and Shellfish

Indians make full use of their food from the sea. Along the southern Coromandel and Malabar coastlines fish and seafood form a major part of the diet. Fish cookery there is imaginative and delightful. Predictably, spices are incorporated in most recipes, either in sauces or tasty marinades. More surprising is the diversity of types of fish available in India, over 2000, and the variety of methods of preparation.

The most popular fish eaten in India include pomfret, rahu, singhara and tingra. These exotic sounding varieties are unavailable here but cod, plaice, herring, mackerel, sea bream, sea bass, halibut, trout, and hake all make good substitutes.

Prawns, lobster, crab, oysters, mussels and cockles all have their place in Indian cookery and thanks to refrigeration and improved transport systems these fruits of the sea are more widely available to the central Indian population. The clear mountain rivers of the north boast excellent freshwater fish, particularly Indian salmon and trout.

In southern India fish often forms the main ingredient of the meal and also makes very good barbecue fare for informal gatherings. The intense heat cooks the fish quickly while retaining its flavour and succulence. Although the recipes given here only show a few of the many methods of dealing with fish, there should be something to suit everybody and all occasions. Adopt and adapt and your palate will be richly rewarded.

Tuna Fish Mollee

The mollee dishes of South India and Sri Lanka have coconut as their base and the meat, fish or vegetable used is usually pre-cooked. Although the types of fish that are normally used are not obtainable here, tinned tuna gives good, quick, results. Serve with fried Bombay duck, rice and a vegetable dish.

200 g (7½ oz) tinned tuna
1 fresh coconut or 1 oz creamed coconut
25 g (1 oz) ghee or butter
1 onion, chopped
3 fresh green chillies, chopped
1 teaspoon turmeric
1 tablespoon chopped parsley
3 hard-boiled eggs

Drain the tuna and break into chunks. Set on one side.
Break open the coconut by hitting it with a hammer. Prize out the flesh and grate it into a bowl. Pour 600 ml (1 pt) of boiling water over and stand for ½ hour. Strain the liquid into a jug, pressing all the moisture out of the flesh. Discard the flesh. If using creamed coconut, dissolve in 600 ml (1 pt) boiling water.
Heat the butter and fry the onion and chillies until soft but not coloured. Sprinkle in the turmeric and then cook for ½ minute. Pour in the coconut liquid and bring to the boil. Simmer uncovered until the liquid has reduced by about half. Add the tuna chunks with the chopped parsley and simmer for another 5-10 minutes.
Cut the hard-boiled eggs into quarters and add these in to the pan towards the end of the cooking time. Stir gently to avoid breaking up the eggs.

Spiced Fried Fish

Variations of this recipe are eaten all over India and different fish are used according to local specialities. Around the coastline pomfret are the favourite; inland freshwater trout and salmon might be treated similarly. A quick and tasty supper dish, it is delicious served with rice, chappaties and a vegetable dish.

675 g (1½ lb) whole fish, cleaned, or prepared fish fillets
2 teaspoons cumin seeds
1 teaspoon fennel seeds
1 teaspoon garam masala
pinch of salt
2 teaspoons paprika
1 tablespoon chopped coriander leaves
1 lemon
50 g (2 oz) flour
oil for shallow frying

Heat a heavy-bottomed pan and scatter in the cumin and fennel seeds. Wait until they just darken slightly in colour then remove and grind them. Place the ground seeds in a bowl and add the garam masala, salt, paprika, coriander leaves and the juice from the lemon. Mix together then pour this over the fish and leave to marinade for 1-2 hours.
Lift the fish out of the bowl and let any liquid drip off them. Dip them into the flour then fry them in the oil in batches for about 5 minutes on each side.

Ginger Prawns

This is a delicious way to serve prawns, but as it is rather rich it is best served as an accompaniment to a main dish. Try ginger prawns with chicken dupiaza or spiced fried fish and pullau rice.

2 cloves garlic, crushed
75 g (3 oz) ghee or butter
2 tablespoons grated fresh tender ginger
1 teaspoon turmeric
1-2 teaspoons paprika
salt and pepper to taste
350 g (12 oz) peeled prawns

Fry the garlic gently in the ghee or butter with the ginger. After a couple of minutes stir in the turmeric, paprika, salt and pepper and cook for 3 minutes.
Add the prawns, cover the pan and cook gently for 10 minutes, shaking the pan occasionally.
Shake the pan over the heat for another minute with the lid off, check the seasoning and then the dish is ready to serve.

Spiced Fried Red Mullet.

Prawn Kofta

These minced prawn balls are cooked in a simple sauce flavoured with tomato and tamarind. They can be served with spiced fried fish, rice, chappaties or parathas and pickles.

275 g (10 oz) prawns
1 onion, finely chopped
1 dessertspoon grated fresh ginger
2 teaspoons curry powder
1 tablespoon flour
1 dessertspoon parsley, finely chopped
½ teaspoon chilli powder (optional)
1 egg, beaten

Place all the ingredients in a liquidizer, except the egg. Blend with just enough egg to bind the mixture together. Shape into small balls and roll lightly in flour.

Sauce
walnut-sized piece of tamarind
3 teaspoons oil
1 onion, chopped
2 cloves garlic, crushed
1 teaspoon garam masala
397 g (14 oz) can of tomatoes
25 g (1 oz) creamed coconut
1-2 tablespoons lemon juice
small bunch of coriander

Soak the tamarind in 150 ml (¼ pt) of boiling water for ½ hour, then strain off the liquid. Discard any bits left in the sieve.

Heat the oil and fry the onion with the garlic and garam masala. Chop the tinned tomatoes and add them to the pan with the tamarind water, creamed coconut and lemon juice. Bring to the boil and simmer for 15 minutes. Season with salt and pepper. Slide the prawn balls into the sauce and simmer very gently for 15 minutes, taking care not to break the balls up. Garnish with coriander.

Spiced Prawn and Egg

This is quick and simple to prepare and is always very popular. Fresh prawns do have more flavour than frozen ones, but tend to be more expensive. Fresh shrimps would be excellent in this dish if you have time to shell them. If you do use frozen prawns or shrimps be sure to let them thaw out on their own (it takes an hour or two) rather than run them under the cold tap. Although they thaw out very quickly this way they lose every bit of flavour and end up tasting like cardboard.

1 onion, finely chopped
2 cloves garlic, crushed
2 chillies, sliced
50 g (2 oz) ghee or butter
1 teaspoon turmeric
1 teaspoon coriander
1 dessertspoon tomato purée
25 g (1 oz) creamed coconut
350 g (12 oz) peeled prawns
1 lemon
4 hard-boiled eggs

Fry the onion, garlic and chillies in the ghee or butter for 3-4 minutes then stir in the turmeric and coriander. Cook for another 3 minutes then add the tomato purée, creamed coconut and 175 ml (6 fl oz) of water. Bring to the boil, stirring all the time, then add the prawns. Squeeze the juice from half of the lemon and pour this into the pan. Simmer the mixture gently for 15 minutes during which time the liquid should thicken a little.

Cut the eggs into quarters lengthwise and put them into the pan.

Check the seasoning and add salt and more lemon juice if required. Stir to coat the eggs, but take care not to break them up. Serve with rice and chappaties.

Indian-Style Fish in Tomato Sauce

Spiced Prawn and Egg (left); Lobster Dupiaza (right).

As this is a fairly wet dish, choose some dry vegetables and plenty of rice to accompany it.

8 fillets of plaice
2 teaspoons cumin seeds
4 tablespoons oil
1 teaspoon black mustard seeds
1 large onion, sliced
3 cloves garlic, crushed
1 dessertspoon grated fresh ginger
½ teaspoon salt
2 teaspoons turmeric
1 teaspoon garam masala
397 g (14 oz) can of tomatoes
1 dessertspoon tomato purée
3 hard-boiled eggs

Wash the fish and cut into thin strips. Set on one side. Heat a heavy pan and add the cumin seeds. When they begin to turn brown tip them out and grind them to a powder.

Heat the oil in a large shallow, lidded pan and fry the mustard seeds until they pop. Stir in the onion, garlic and ginger along with the ground cumin, salt, turmeric and garam masala. Stir over a medium heat for 5 minutes.

Carefully stir in the fish, mixing well to coat with the spices, but taking care not to break up the fillets. Cook for 5 minutes then remove the fish only with a slotted spoon.

Quickly add the tomatoes and tomato purée to the pan and bring to the boil. Boil rapidly for 5-6 minutes then blend until smooth in a liquidizer. Return the sauce to the pan and add the fish. Simmer gently for a further 5-10 minutes. Slice the hard-boiled eggs and use these to garnish the dish.

Lobster Dupiaza

Instead of using all lobster you can make up half of the quantity with prawns. Serve with plenty of rice, soft nan and hot lemon or lime pickle.

2 large onions
50 g (2 oz) ghee or butter
1 tablespoon grated fresh ginger
1 clove garlic, crushed
½ teaspoon salt
2 tablespoons oil
3 teaspoons ground cumin
1½ teaspoons ground coriander
1 teaspoon garam masala
2 cloves
350 g (12 oz) lobster meat
juice of 1 lemon
85 ml (3 fl oz) plain yoghurt

Chop one of the onions roughly and fry in the ghee or butter with the ginger and garlic. Do this over a low heat with the lid on to keep the onions soft. When they begin to brown remove them from the pan with a slotted spoon and blend to a purée in a liquidizer with the salt.

Add the rest of the ghee or butter to the pan and sprinkle in the cumin, coriander, garam masala and cloves. Stir-fry them for a minute then add the onion purée, lobster and lemon juice.

Meanwhile slice the other onion very finely and fry in the oil until brown and crispy.

Stir the yoghurt into the lobster mixture, spoon into a serving dish and scatter the fried onions over the top.

Baked Mackerel

The mackerel are marinaded in a tangy spiced mixture which really complements the rather oily fish. Serve them with rice, dhal and poppadums.

4 mackerel
1 large lemon
1½ teaspoons paprika
1 dessertspoon grated fresh ginger
1 clove garlic, crushed
2 teaspoons garam masala
¼ teaspoon salt

Clean the fish and remove the heads and tails (or ask your fishmonger to do this for you). Rinse and dry with kitchen paper. Cut three diagonal slashes on each side of the fishes.

Squeeze the juice from the lemon and pour it into a bowl. Add all the remaining ingredients to the bowl. Mix well then pour over the fish, making sure the marinade also gets inside the fish. Leave, covered for 6-12 hours in the refrigerator.

Wrap the mackerel in foil and bake for ½ hour in a hot oven, Gas Mark 7, 215°C, 420°F. Open up the foil and pour off any liquid. Bake, uncovered for a further 5 minutes to crisp the skin a little and you will have tasty, succulent fish.

Cashew-Stuffed Trout

This stuffing mixture can be used with a variety of fish, but tastes especially good with trout. These would form the main dish for a meal and might be accompanied by pullau rice, a vegetable dish and chutneys.

4 trout, cleaned
1 large onion, finely chopped
2 green chillies, finely chopped
40 g (1½ oz) ghee or butter
2 tablespoons chopped coriander leaves
100 g (4 oz) ground almonds
175 g (6 oz) unsalted cashew nuts
1 teaspoon turmeric
¼ teaspoon salt
½ lemon
3 tablespoons oil

Clean the trout by slitting open the bellies from head to tail and removing the innards. Using a pair of scissors, snip through the back bone close to the head and gently ease the bone out all the way down the fish. Have a sharp knife in your other hand and use it to free the bone from the flesh as you lift it out. Snip through the bone as close to the tail as you can. Open the fish out and check that all the bones have come away with the back bone (your fishmonger may be able to do this for you). Meanwhile, set the fish on one side while you prepare the stuffing.

Fry the onion and chillies in the butter. When they have softened stir in the coriander, ground almonds and cashew nuts and turmeric. Season with salt and stir over a moderate heat for 5 minutes. Squeeze the juice from the lemon and pour it into the pan. Continue to cook until the mixture is dry, remove from the heat and allow to cool. If you are not cooking the trout immediately, make sure the stuffing is completely cold before you add it to the fish.

Cashew-Stuffed Trout.

Open the trout and spoon the mixture down the centres. Fold the fish back to their normal shape and tie them with thread to hold the stuffing in place.

If you have a shallow frying pan that is big enough to take the fish use it to fry the trout in the oil for about 8 minutes on each side. Alternatively place the fish on a sheet of oiled foil and grill the fish for the same length of time. These fish also barbecue very well. Take care not to break them when turning them.

East Coast Fish

Traditionally this dish uses up to 8 dried red chillies. I have reduced the number to 2 or 3 but if you like chillies try it with more. Leave the chillies whole so that they can be removed before serving.

450 g (1 lb) filleted cod
25 g (1 oz) ghee or butter
1 onion, finely sliced
2 cloves of crushed garlic
2 teaspoons ground coriander
2-3 dried red chillies
1 teaspoon turmeric
1 lemon
4 tomatoes, quartered
½ teaspoon salt
small bunch of coriander leaves

Cut the fish into large pieces. Heat the ghee or butter in a pan and fry the onion and garlic with the coriander, whole chillies and turmeric.

Add 300 ml (½ pt) of water and the juice of the lemon. Bring to the boil, add the tomatoes and simmer for 10 minutes. Add the fish with a pinch of salt, cover the pan and simmer gently for 10-15 minutes or until the fish is cooked. Remove the red chillies and garnish with coriander leaves.

Tandoori Fish

This is such a simple and delicious way of preparing fish that I am sure it will become one of your favourite dishes.

1 k (2 lb) whole fish such as mullet or mackerel
175 ml plain yoghurt
1 tablespoon grated fresh ginger
1 teaspoon paprika
½ teaspoon salt
2 tablespoons lemon juice
1 tablespoon ground coriander
1 teaspoon garam masala
1 clove garlic, crushed
few drops red food colouring (optional)

Clean the fish and wipe inside and out with kitchen paper. Cut slits diagonally in the skin, then place the fish in a bowl.

Combine all the other ingredients and pour them over the fish. Make sure that the marinade coats both the inside and outside of the fish. Cover the bowl and leave in the fridge for 24 hours.

Heat the oven to its maximum setting and oil the bars of one of the oven racks. Place a baking tray under the oiled rack to catch the drips. Place the fish on the rack and spoon some of the marinade over. Bake for 15 minutes, turning and basting with the marinade every 5 minutes.

The fish can be cooked with great success on a barbecue.

Bombay Duck with Tomato and Aubergine

Bombay duck is the popular name for the bombloe fish caught in the waters around Bombay. They got this nickname from their habit of swimming very close to the surface of the water. They are sold dried and salted and are obtainable here in Indian shops and delicatessens. If the taste is too salty for you, soak the 'ducks' in cold water for ½ hour before cooking.

100 g (4 oz) Bombay duck
1 aubergine (eggplant)
1 onion, chopped
2 dried red chillies, chopped
6 tablespoons oil
2 teaspoons turmeric
1 teaspoon cumin
1 teaspoon ground coriander
4 tomatoes, quartered
juice of 1 lime
small bunch coriander leaves

Snap the Bombay duck in half. Wash the aubergine and cut it into small chunks. Fry the onion and chillies in the oil for 5 minutes. Stir in the turmeric, cumin and coriander and chunks of aubergine. Keep stirring until the aubergine begins to brown on all sides (about 10 minutes).

Add the tomatoes and 300 ml (½ pt) of water. Simmer for a further 10 minutes. Add the lime juice to the pan with the Bombay duck. Cook uncovered for 10 minutes, adding water if it becomes too dry.

Spoon into a serving dish and garnish with coriander leaves.

Prawn and Potato Curry

This curry is quick to prepare and the addition of potatoes makes it fairly filling. Eat it with yellow lemon rice, coconut curry and bhindi bhaji for a tasty supper.

walnut-sized piece of tamarind or 1 lemon
3 tablespoons oil
1 teaspoon poppy seeds
1 teaspoon black mustard seeds
2 teaspoons ground cumin
1½ teaspoons turmeric
1 tablespoon grated fresh ginger
1 clove garlic, crushed
pinch of asafoetida (optional)
450 g (1 lb) cooked baby new potatoes or large diced potatoes
350 g (12 oz) prawns
1 tablespoon chopped parsley

Soak the tamarind in 300 ml (½ pt) of boiling water. Leave to stand for 10 minutes then strain the liquid and discard any bits. If using the lemon, squeeze the juice and make up to 300 ml (½ pt) with cold water.

Heat the oil and add the poppy and mustard seeds. Cook until they pop then stir in the cumin, turmeric, ginger, garlic and asafoetida.

After a couple of minutes add the potatoes and mix well. Pour in the liquid and bring to the boil. Let the mixture bubble away until it has reduced by about half its volume. Add the prawns and a pinch of salt and simmer gently for 10-12 minutes. Sprinkle in the chopped parsley and transfer to a serving dish.

Prawn Bhajis

Bhajis can be eaten as a snack with chutney or served as part of a meal. They are best eaten freshly cooked, but extra batter mixture can be stored, covered, in the fridge for 24 hours.

50 g (2 oz) self-raising flour
50 g (2 oz) chickpea flour (also known as gram flour or besan)
½ teaspoon salt
1 teaspoon turmeric
½ teaspoon paprika
2 small eggs, beaten
1 fresh green chilli, finely chopped
1 tablespoon onion, finely chopped
100 g (4 oz) chopped prawns
½ teaspoon garam masala
oil for deep frying

Sieve the flours, salt, turmeric and paprika into a bowl. Stir the eggs into the flour. Add the chilli to the batter with the onion, prawns and garam masala.

Heat the oil in a deep frying pan and when hot drop a few teaspoons of the mixture in and fry until golden brown. Remove with a slotted spoon and continue until all the mixture is used up.

Crab with Toasted Coconut

This recipe comes from Kerala, on the southwestern coast. Seafood and coconuts are abundant, and this combination of delicate crab and crunchy coconut is well worth trying.

2 onions, chopped
1 clove garlic, crushed
1 teaspoon grated fresh ginger
50 g (2 oz) ghee or butter
2 teaspoons ground coriander
½-1 teaspoon chilli powder
1 teaspoon turmeric
walnut-sized piece of tamarind
25 g (1 oz) creamed coconut
1 tablespoon red lentils
350 g (12 oz) crab meat
salt to taste
125 ml (4 fl oz) cream
25 g (1 oz) desiccated or unsweetened shredded coconut

Fry the onion and the garlic with the ginger in the ghee or butter for 1 minute then cover the pan and allow them to sweat gently for 2-3 minutes. Stir in the coriander, chilli and turmeric and cook briskly, stirring all the time.

Meanwhile, pour 300 ml (½ pt) of boiling water over the tamarind and let it stand for 10 minutes. Strain out any bits and pour the hot liquid into the pan with the creamed coconut. Sprinkle in the lentils and bring the mixture to the boil. Allow it to boil for 5 minutes to soften the lentils, then reduce the heat to its lowest setting.

Add the crab and simmer gently for 15 minutes.

Toast the coconut under the grill until golden and crunchy.

Just before serving, check the seasoning and add a little salt if necessary then fold in the cream, taking care not to crush the crab. Tip into a serving bowl and sprinkle the top with the coconut.

Crab with Toasted Coconut (top): Prawn and Potato Curry.

Meat Dishes

Of all the meats, goat and mutton are the most popular in India; neither of these are easily available to us. Lamb is the nearest substitute and this has been suggested for most of the recipes in this section. Often types of meat can be interchanged, and when you have tried beef vindaloo, for example, you may like to experiment using pork.

Generally lean meat is favoured, so trim away excess fat. Meat can be left on the bone but if so increase the amount given in the recipe by about one third.

When frying meat do not overpack the pan. Cook in batches using just enough meat to fit comfortably into the base of the pan, and fry over a medium to high heat. Unless the meat is sealed quickly in this manner the juices will flow from the meat so that it begins to simmer in liquid rather than fry. The meat will brown when fried, giving a richer colour to the dish, and it helps keep the meat succulent.

Where a meat dish is covered and simmered on the hob, keep the heat very low or the meat will burn on the base of the pan and the liquid will boil, making the meat tough. If you find difficulty getting a low enough temperature it would be better to cook the dish in the oven at about Gas Mark 3, 150°C or 300°F although the cooking time will be slightly longer.

Ground beef and lamb are used extensively. Buy the best minced beef from your butcher as this will be leaner and tastier. Butchers will often only mince lamb if you order sufficient to make it worthwhile so either put it in a reasonable order and freeze the surplus or mince the meat at home yourself. If using a food processor for this, do not blend for too long at a time; instead give it several short bursts of power until the meat is the required consistency.

The use of yoghurt in meat cooking serves two purposes. When meat is marinaded in a yoghurt and spice mixture, the yoghurt will help the flavourings penetrate the flesh and act as a tenderizer. When it is added to a dish in the final stages, yoghurt tones down the strength of the spices and creates a creamy sauce. Once again feel free to reduce (or increase) the amount of chillies, paprika or cayenne pepper used.

Roghan Josh

This is a famous dish dating back to the Mogul Empire. Traditionally, it would have been made with mutton, but lamb is also acceptable. As Roghan Josh is very rich serve it with plain rice, nan, a crisp vegetable dish or salad, and a celery and walnut raita.

3 tablespoons oil
25 g (1 oz) ghee or butter
5 cloves
1 teaspoon ground ginger
1 dessertspoon grated fresh ginger
small stick of cinnamon
pinch of asafoetida (optional)
6 cracked green cardamom pods
2 tablespoons finely chopped onion
4 cloves garlic, crushed
1 k (2 lb) diced leg of lamb
175 ml (6 fl oz) plain yoghurt
4 tomatoes
few strands of saffron
25 g (1 oz) ground almonds

Heat the oil and ghee or butter in a large frying pan and add the ground and fresh ginger, cinnamon, asafoetida, cardamom, onion and garlic. Fry these ingredients for a moment then add some of the diced lamb. Stir over a moderate heat until brown, then remove the meat and continue to fry until all the meat has been fried in the spices.

Put all the meat back into the pan, or if this is a tight fit, transfer everything to a large saucepan. Add 2 tablespoons of yoghurt, stir well and cook until the mixture is dry (about 5 minutes). Continue to add a little yoghurt at a time until it has all been incorporated.

Cut the tomatoes into thick slices and add them to the pan. Cover and cook for 10 minutes, stirring occasionally.

Meanwhile soak the saffron in 450 ml (¾ pt) of boiled water, then add to the pan. Cover and simmer very gently for 1¼ hours or until the meat is tender. Stir in the ground almonds and cook uncovered to reduce the sauce to a thick clinging consistency. Season with a little salt before serving.

Spicy Stuffed Capsicums

This dish can be made with left-over cooked lamb or beef. If you use a food processor to mince the meat, do not over-work it or the result will be pulpy and completely textureless. It is best to give several short bursts of power to ensure that all the meat receives equal treatment.

4 green or sweet red peppers
2 tablespoons oil
2 teaspoons garam masala
1 teaspoon ground cumin
1 fresh green chilli, deseeded and sliced
1 teaspoon turmeric
1 teaspoon grated fresh ginger
2 cloves of garlic, finely chopped
1 large onion, finely chopped
½ k (1 lb) cooked mince meat
½ teaspoon salt
2 large tomatoes, quartered
250 ml (8 fl oz) meat stock or water
75 g (3 oz) flaked almonds

Wash the peppers and cut off the stalk end to make a cap. Carefully cut out the stalk, remove the seeds and pith, then blanch in boiling water for 2 minutes. Drain and hold under cold water, redrain and set on one side.

Heat the oil and fry the garam masala, cumin, chilli and turmeric for 1 minute. Add the ginger, garlic, onion and meat to the pan. Fry briskly for 10 minutes, stirring all the time. Add the salt and the tomatoes to the mixture. Pour the stock or water over, bring to the boil then simmer until the liquid has all evaporated. Stir in the flaked almonds.

Fill the capsicums with the meat mixture and replace the caps on top. Stand upright in an ovenproof dish and bake for 20 minutes at Gas Mark 5, 200°C, 400°F.

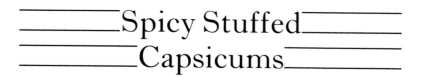

Roghan Josh.

Spicy Lamb and Lentil

This is a nourishing dish to which I have added peas to make it more colourful. It should be cooked until thick then served with chappaties or parathas, rice and vegetables. Crisp bhajis or poppadums would add bite to the meal.

walnut-sized piece of tamarind
2 large onions, sliced
3 cloves garlic, sliced
2-3 teaspoons home-mixed curry powder
4 tablespoons oil
¾ k (1½ lb) diced lean lamb
175 g (6 oz) lentils
100 g (4 oz) peas
1 tablespoon chopped fresh coriander leaves
salt

Soak the tamarind in a little boiling water for 10 minutes then strain, pushing the pulp through and discarding any bits. Make the liquid up to ¾ l (1½ pts) by adding more water.

Fry the onions, garlic and curry powder in the oil, then add some of the lamb. Cook quickly until the meat is brown and sealed. Remove the meat with a slotted spoon and continue in this fashion until all the meat has been used up.

Transfer the meat and spices to a larger pan if necessary, stir in the lentils and pour over the tamarind liquid. Cover and simmer for 1 hour. Add the peas, coriander leaves and a little salt and continue to cook until the meat is tender and the sauce is thick. Stir gently to prevent the lentils burning on the bottom of the pan and add a little more water if needed.

Seek Kebab

Seek Kebabs are quick to prepare and cook. Miniature kebabs threaded onto cocktail sticks can be served as party food, though they can be a bit fiddly to make. For supper serve kebabs with pullau rice, a couple of moist dishes (a vegetable and dhal perhaps), lemon or lime pickle and some raw sliced salad vegetables.

½ k (1 lb) minced lean beef or lamb
25 g (1 oz) butter, softened
25 g (1 oz) plain flour or gram flour
1 egg yolk, lightly beaten
2 teaspoons ground coriander
1 tablespoon chopped fresh coriander
1 teaspoon ground sesame seeds
½ teaspoon ground fenugreek seeds
½ teaspoon chilli powder or paprika
½ teaspoon ground ginger
3 cloves garlic, crushed
grated rind of 1 lemon
salt and freshly ground black pepper
1 onion, grated or finely chopped

Combine all the ingredients in a large bowl and knead by hand until well mixed and stiff.

Grease some metal skewers. Divide the meat mixture into 6-8 equal portions. Flatten each portion in the palm of the hand and wrap around the centre of a skewer. Press and mould the meat to make tapering sausage shapes.

Cook under a hot grill, turning frequently until the outside is golden brown.

Maharashtran Mutton

Mutton is very popular throughout India. If it is difficult to buy then use diced leg of lamb. A wok or Indian kadhai is useful for frying large amounts of meat as they have a greater usable surface area than a frying pan.

1 k (2 lb) diced mutton
1 tablespoon grated fresh ginger
2 cloves garlic, crushed
2 teaspoons turmeric
½ teaspoon salt
4 tablespoons oil
2 teaspoons poppy seeds
1 tablespoon whole coriander seeds
1 teaspoon ground cumin
1 clove
1-2 dried red chillies, chopped
1 onion, sliced
3 tablespoons water
25 g (1 oz) creamed coconut
150 ml (¼ pt) plain yoghurt
1 teaspoon garam masala
small bunch fresh coriander

Lamb with Fenugreek

This is a delicately flavoured dish. It can be dressed up for special occasions by adding quartered hard boiled eggs, fried almonds and raisins or by stirring in a couple of tablespoons of cream at the last minute. Fenugreek seeds burn easily so take care when frying them.

4 tablespoons oil
½ teaspoon mustard seeds
½ teaspoon paprika
½ teaspoon fenugreek seeds
2 teaspoons ground coriander
1 teaspoon turmeric
pinch of asafoetida (optional)
1 dessertspoon grated fresh ginger
2 large onions, sliced
4 lamb chump chops
25 g (1 oz) unsweetened desiccated coconut or freshly grated coconut
150 ml (¼ pt) buttermilk
2 tablespoons chopped fenugreek leaves
salt
¼–½ teaspoon garam masala
few fenugreek leaves for garnishing

Heat the oil and fry the mustard seeds, keeping the pan covered until they have stopped popping. Sprinkle in the paprika, fenugreek seeds, coriander, turmeric and asafoetida, if using. Cook for ½ minute then add the ginger and onions and cook gently until the onions are soft.

Turn up the heat, lay in the chops and fry for 5 minutes on each side. Stir in the coconut, buttermilk, chopped fenugreek leaves and a dash of salt. Lower the heat, cover tightly and cook for 20 minutes, shaking the pan occasionally.

Serve sprinkled with garam masala and a few fenugreek leaves.

Lamb Tikka Kebabs

These kebabs can either be barbecued or grilled. They are quick to prepare, but should be left to marinate overnight. If fresh mint is not available, add the grated rind of an orange rather than dried mint.

1 lemon
1 tablespoon grated fresh ginger
1 onion, finely minced
2 teaspoons ground coriander
1 tablespoon fresh mint leaves, finely chopped
2 cloves of garlic, crushed
1 teaspoon salt
½ teaspoon ground cardamom seeds
300 ml (½ pt) thick plain yoghurt
¾ k (1½ lb) evenly diced leg of lamb

Grate the rind from the lemon and squeeze the juice from the flesh. Mix all the ingredients together to make a marinade and pour this over the lamb. Cover and leave for 12–24 hours, stirring occasionally.

Lightly oil some skewers and thread the lamb pieces onto them, leaving a space between each. Heat the grill to its maximum temperature. Cover a baking tray with aluminium foil and lay the kebabs on top.

Grill for approximately 20 minutes, basting frequently with the marinade and turning the kebabs once or twice. When ready, the outside of the meat should be well browned and crusty and the middle moist and faintly pink.

To barbecue the kebabs, lay them directly onto the rack and cook them in the same manner.

Spicy Lamb and Lentil (left); *Lamb with Fenugreek* (right).

Trim the meat and place in a large bowl. Stir in the ginger, garlic, turmeric and salt. Leave to stand for 1 hour, stirring occasionally.

In a large frying pan, wok or kadhai heat the oil and sprinkle in the poppy and coriander seeds. Cover the pan and cook until the coriander seeds have finished 'popping' then stir in the cumin, clove, chillies and onion slices. Add just enough meat to cover the surface of the pan and fry briskly until coated with the spices and sealed. Remove the meat with a slotted spoon and stir-fry the meat in batches.

Pour 3 tablespoons of boiling water over the creamed coconut. Stir until it has dissolved then mix with 3 tablespoons of the yoghurt.

Put all the meat back into the pan with half of the coconut mixture and cook until the pan is dry. Add the remaining coconut mixture and when dry transfer either to a lidded saucepan or a flameproof casserole dish. Pour 450 ml (¾ pt) of water over the meat and bring to the boil. Cover the pan and simmer very slowly or bake at Gas mark 3 (170°C, 325°F) or until the meat is tender (about 1 hour). Stir in the garam masala and 1 tablespoon of chopped coriander leaves and cook for a further 5 minutes.

Turn out onto a serving dish, spoon the remaining yoghurt over the top and decorate with the rest of the coriander leaves.

Beef Vindaloo

Beef Vindaloo.

Pork is the traditional meat used for vindaloos, but beef is also good. All vindaloo recipes use vinegar and adopt a liberal approach towards chillies. Although the character of the dish is changed, it is quite all right to reduce the number of chillies to suit your palate.

1 tablespoon whole coriander seeds
2 teaspoons whole cumin seeds
3 onions, roughly chopped
4 cloves garlic, crushed
½ teaspoon fenugreek seeds
3 dried red chillies
1 teaspoon turmeric
1 tablespoon grated fresh ginger
125 ml (4 fl oz) wine vinegar
1 k (2 lb) steak
1 bay leaf
5 tablespoons oil
salt to taste

Dry roast the coriander and cumin seeds until they are brittle but not burnt. Pound them with pestle and mortar or grind in a coffee grinder. Put the onions and garlic into a liquidizer with the freshly ground cumin and coriander, fenugreek seeds, chillies, turmeric, ginger and wine vinegar. Blend to a smooth paste.

Cut the meat into even cubes and place in a large bowl with the bay leaf. Pour the vinegar marinade over and mix well. Cover and leave in the refrigerator for at least 12 hours, stirring once or twice.

Heat the oil in a large frying pan. Lift some of the meat into the pan, using a slotted spoon to drain off any surplus vinegar. When the meat has browned remove from the pan and add the next batch. Carry on until all the meat has been sealed in hot oil.

Transfer the meat to a casserole dish, pour over any remaining marinade along with just enough water to cover the meat. Cook, covered for 2 hours at Gas Mark 3, 150°C, 300°F or until the meat is tender.

Season with a little salt and turn into a serving dish. Fiery dishes like the vindaloo are usually allowed to cool for at least 5-10 minutes before eating them as they can be overpowering.

Curried Beef and Capsicum

This dish looks pretty if you use a mixture of red, green and yellow peppers. It has a pleasant tangy flavour and is quite mild. Serve it with pullau rice, dhal, poppadums and mango chutney.

small piece of pressed tamarind
1 dessertspoon honey
3 tablespoons vinegar
1 teaspoon ground turmeric
1 tablespoon tomato purée
1 tablespoon ground coriander
½-1 teaspoon paprika
pinch of asafoetida (optional)
1 teaspoon mustard seeds
1 onion, thinly sliced
2 tablespoons oil
1 tablespoon grated fresh ginger
¾ k (1½ lb) lean steak cut into thin strips
large pinch of salt
3 small peppers

Pour 450 ml (¾ pt) of boiling water over the tamarind. Leave to soak for 10 minutes then strain into a jug, pushing the soft pulp through the sieve. Discard any bits left in the sieve. Stir in the honey then set on one side.

Next prepare a spicy paste by mixing the vinegar with the turmeric, tomato purée, coriander, paprika and asafoetida.

Gently fry the mustard seeds and onion in the oil. Add the grated ginger and the vinegar paste and cook for 1 minute. Mix in the strips of beef and cook for 15 minutes or until well browned. Add the salt and pour in the tamarind liquid.

Transfer the contents of the pan into a casserole dish and cook in the centre of a moderate oven (Gas Mark 4, 180°C, 350°F) for 1 hour. Slice the capsicums and discard the seeds and white pith. Stir these into the curry and continue to cook for another 30 minutes or until the meat is tender.

Meat Mollee

Mollees are South Indian dishes and all feature coconut in one form or another. For convenience the recipe uses creamed coconut mixed to a thin paste with cooking liquid, but traditionally 'coconut milk' is used. To make this you will need to crack open a coconut and grate the fresh flesh into a bowl. Cover this with 300 ml (½ pt) of boiling water and leave overnight to infuse. Next day strain the liquid and coconut through muslin, squeezing out all the moisture. Use this liquid in your cooking.

2 large onions, sliced
3 tablespoons oil
1 k (2 lb) diced lean lamb or beef
6 peppercorns
1 clove
25 g (1 oz) creamed coconut or 300 ml (½ pt) coconut milk (see above)
1 teaspoon mustard seeds
½ teaspoon fenugreek seeds
1-2 teaspoons chilli powder
3 cloves of garlic, crushed
1 teaspoon ground cardamom

Fry one onion in 1 tablespoon of oil until soft. Put this with the meat, peppercorns, clove and enough water to cover in a flameproof casserole dish and cook in a moderate oven (Gas Mark 4, 180°C, 350°F) for about 1 hour or until tender.

Lift the meat and liquor out of the casserole dish while still hot and set on one side. Strain the cooking liquor and mix 300 ml (½ pt) with the creamed coconut.

Heat the remaining oil in the casserole and fry the mustard seeds until they pop (keep the pan covered until the popping stops) then add the fenugreek seeds, the remaining onion, chilli powder, crushed garlic and cardamom.

Cook for a couple of minutes then stir in the cooked meat and liquor. Stir this mixture over a high heat for 15 minutes then pour over the coconut liquid. Simmer uncovered for 10 minutes. Check the seasoning for salt before serving.

This dish can be made using leftover cooked meat. It is also excellent if cooked the day before then reheated thoroughly before eating the next day.

Spicy Kofta and Egg

Koftas are meat balls usually made with minced lamb or beef, variously spiced and cooked in flavoured sauces. Because they are both cheap and quick to make they are good everyday fare. The different types of koftas are limitless, this recipe is rather a simple one but you can invent your own speciality by varying the meat and spices used. Koftas are sometimes cooked in coconut milk or buttermilk.

2 medium onions
2 cloves garlic, crushed
½ k (1 lb) minced lean beef
½ teaspoon ground cumin
1 teaspoon turmeric
¼ teaspoon ground mace
pinch of freshly grated nutmeg
1 egg, lightly beaten
2 teaspoons home-mixed curry powder (see page 11)
25 g (1 oz) ghee or butter
397 g (14 oz) can tomatoes, pushed through a sieve
salt to taste
3 hard-boiled eggs
3 tablespoons plain yoghurt
fresh coriander leaves to garnish

Grate one onion into a bowl or mince in a food processor. Lightly beat the egg. Add the garlic, beef, cumin, turmeric, mace, nutmeg and half of the beaten egg to the grated onion. Knead by hand until the mixture is thoroughly blended and stiff. Form into small balls (about 2 cm/1 inch in diameter) and put aside on a wet plate while you prepare the sauce.

Chop the remaining onion and gently fry with the curry powder in the ghee or butter until the onion is softened but not brown. Add the sieved tomatoes. Season with a little salt and simmer for 10 minutes.

Pour the sauce into a shallow ovenproof dish and carefully slide in the koftas. Cover the dish and bake for 45 minutes at Gas Mark 4, 180°C or 360°F.

Shell the hard-boiled eggs and cut them into wedges. Tuck them in between the koftas and cook for a further 5 minutes to ensure that the eggs are thoroughly heated.

Spoon the yoghurt over the Kofta and egg and decorate with some fresh coriander leaves just before taking the dish to the table. Serve directly from the dish.

Keema

This is a useful standby and makes a tasty supper dish. Depending on what you want to serve with the Keema you can alter the consistency to suit, although Keema is most often cooked until almost all the liquid has evaporated and you are left with juicy meat topped with crunchy nuts.

1-2 fresh green chillies
½ teaspoon ground cumin
1 teaspoon ground coriander
½ teaspoon ground ginger
1 teaspoon turmeric
¼ teaspoon ground mace or small piece of blade mace
4-5 tablespoons oil
¾ k (1½ lb) minced lean beef
2 onions, finely sliced
3 cloves garlic, crushed
397 g (14 oz) can tomatoes
½ teaspoon salt
50 g (2 oz) flaked almonds
50 g (2 oz) raisins
15 g (½ oz) ghee or butter

Chop the chillies, discarding the seeds. Fry the cumin, coriander, ginger, turmeric and mace in the oil for 1 minute then stir in the meat, onion, garlic and chillies. Stir-fry for 10 minutes or until the meat is well browned.

Roughly chop the tomatoes and add to the pan with their juice and the salt. Bring to the boil, cover and simmer gently for 30 to 40 minutes. For a drier consistency remove the lid and cook until some or all of the liquid has evaporated.

When nearly ready fry the nuts and raisins in the ghee or butter, taking care not to burn them. Transfer the Keema to a serving dish and sprinkle the fried fruit and nuts on top.

Mixed Vegetable and Meat Curry

Ideally this curry should be cooked the day before it is required to let the flavours fully impregnate the main ingredients. To reheat, cook in a moderate oven (Gas Mark 4, 180°C, 350°F) for 30-40 minutes. Serve with plain rice, chappaties, dhal and pickle or with crusty bread and salad.

2 large onions, finely chopped
3 cloves of garlic, crushed
1 teaspoon garam masala
50 g (2 oz) ghee or butter
½ k (1 lb) topside of beef, thinly sliced
2 tablespoons oil
1 teaspoon mustard seeds
small stick cinnamon
2 teaspoons turmeric
½-1 teaspoon chilli powder
2 teaspoons ground coriander
1 tablespoon tomato purée
175 g (6 oz) green beans
3 medium potatoes, peeled and sliced
3 carrots, chopped
100 g (4 oz) peas
6 tomatoes, quartered
salt to taste

Fry half the onions and garlic with the garam masala in half the ghee or butter. Spread this over the slices of meat and roll up into neat parcels. Tie with string.

Blanch the potatoes and carrots in boiling water for four minutes until they are part cooked. Drain and set on one side.

In a large frying pan heat the remaining ghee or butter and oil. Fry the mustard seeds, cinnamon, turmeric, chilli powder and coriander with the rest of the onion and garlic. Lay the meat rolls on top and cook quickly until they are brown and sealed.

Mix the tomato purée with ½ l (1 pint) of water and pour into the pan. Stir in all the vegetables, bring to the boil, cover tightly and simmer very slowly for 1-1½ hours. During the last ¼ hour remove the lid and let most of the liquid evaporate. This curry can also be cooked in a medium oven, which lessens the danger of it boiling over or burning.

Lamb with Almond Stuffing

Contrary to popular belief, whole joints of meat are roasted in India, usually over an open fire. A gas or electric oven will work well enough and if you have a rotisserie attachment so much the better.
To prevent the meat sitting in its own juices, set the joint on a rack over a roasting tin. Slices of the lamb taste equally good hot or cold, but if the whole piece is to be eaten cold, you should trim away as much fat as possible before cooking.

1 boned loin or shoulder of lamb
4 cloves garlic, slivered
50 g (2 oz) blanched almonds
75 g (3 oz) ghee or butter
½ teaspoon ground ginger
½ teaspoon ground cardamom seeds
1 teaspoon paprika
1½ teaspoons garam masala
2 onions, finely chopped
rind of 1 lemon
25 g (1 oz) ground almonds
1 tablespoon fresh coriander leaves
150 ml (¼ pt) plain yoghurt
pinch of salt
freshly ground pepper

Lay the loin of lamb skin side down or open out the shoulder. With a small, sharp knife, make slits halfway through the meat with the point of the knife and tuck a sliver of garlic and an almond into each one. Crush any remaining garlic and reserve.

Heat two-thirds of the ghee or butter and gently fry the ginger, cardamom, paprika and garam masala with the onion and crushed garlic until the onion is soft. Stir in the lemon rind, ground almonds and the coriander leaves. Spread the mixture over the meat, roll up firmly and tie with string.

Soften the remaining butter and work in the yoghurt, a pinch of salt and pepper and an extra teaspoon of garam masala if liked. Spread some of this mixture over the lamb.

Either thread the meat onto a spit or stand on a rack over a roasting tin and cook for about 1¼ hours at Gas Mark 6, 200°C, 400°F. Turn and baste the meat frequently with the yoghurt mixture and the cooking juices.

Take the meat out of the oven and leave to stand for 5 minutes before untying and slicing.

Lamb with Almond Stuffing.

South Indian Stick Curry

Variations of this simple dish of skewered meat cooked in a spiced sauce are eaten around Madras. The meat 'sticks' can have sliced vegetables threaded onto them as well, if liked. Here finely sliced ginger gives the meat a distinctive flavour. Serve with plenty of plain rice, dhal, poppadums and fresh chutney.

walnut-sized piece of pressed tamarind
¾ k (1½ lb) piece of lean lamb or beef, cut into thin strips
large knob of fresh, tender ginger, thinly sliced
1 onion, chopped
25 g (1 oz) ghee or butter
1 teaspoon ground cumin
2 teaspoons ground coriander
½ teaspoon ground mango powder
1 teaspoon mustard seeds
pinch of paprika
397 g (14 oz) can of tomatoes, chopped

Soak the tamarind in 125 ml (4 fl oz) of boiling water for 10 minutes, then strain. Push the pulp through the sieve and discard any bits.

Thread the meat and ginger alternately onto short wooden skewers (saté skewers are ideal for this and are obtainable from delicatessens) or metal skewers, packing them tightly.

Fry the onion in the ghee or butter with the cumin, coriander, mango powder, mustard and paprika for 2 minutes. Mix the tamarind water with the canned tomatoes and their juice and pour into the pan. Simmer for 10 minutes uncovered then transfer to a casserole dish.

Lay the meat sticks in the tomato sauce, cover and cook in a moderate oven (Gas Mark 4, 180°C, 350°F) for 1 hour to 1½ hours or until tender. The cooking time will vary somewhat depending on the type of meat chosen.

Dry Lamb Curry

Although the lamb in the recipe is cooked in a sauce, towards the end of the cooking time the liquid is reduced until it thickens and just coats the meat. To complement the lamb, serve it with plain rice, green dhal tarka, khumbar mattar, poppadums and chutney.

½ l (1 pt) water
walnut-sized piece of pressed tamarind
2 medium onions
50 g (2 oz) ghee or butter
2 teaspoons turmeric
1 tablespoon ground coriander
1 teaspoon garam masala
1 k (2 lb) lean diced lamb
1 tablespoon ground cumin
5 cloves garlic, crushed
2 tablespoons tomato purée
½ tsp salt

Bring the water to the boil and pour over the tamarind. Soak for 10 minutes then strain, pressing the pulp through the sieve and discarding any bits. Peel and quarter the onions then separate out the layers.

Heat the ghee or butter in a heavy-based pan and fry the turmeric, coriander, garam masala and cumin with the onion and garlic.

Add the meat and fry briskly until it is all sealed and coated with the spices. Do this in two batches if your pan is not large enough to hold all the meat.

Pour in the tamarind water, add the tomato purée and season with salt. Cover the pan and simmer for 1¼ hours or until the meat is tender. Check occasionally and add more water if it appears dry.

If you are losing moisture as steam around the lid, make a more effective seal by covering the pan with aluminium foil, then place the lid on top. When the meat is cooked, remove the lid and cook until the sauce is thick and clinging to the meat, taking care not to let it burn.

44

South Indian Stick Curry (left); *Stuffed Pork Cutlets* (right).

Stuffed Pork Cutlets

These cutlets taste equally delicious served hot or cold. Pop one into a packed lunch and you will never want to eat pork pie again!

4 pork chops
50 g (2 oz) thick cottage cheese
1 tablespoon chopped fresh coriander leaves
salt and freshly ground black pepper
150 ml (¼ pt) thick plain yoghurt
2 cloves garlic, crushed
2 tablespoons lemon juice
pinch of ground cinnamon
½-1 teaspoon paprika
50 g (2 oz) plain flour
1 egg, beaten
40 g (1½ oz) dried breadcrumbs
4 tablespoons oil

Remove the bones from the chops and cover with a sheet of damp greaseproof paper. Hit each chop several times with a rolling pin to flatten slightly. Cut a deep slit into the side of each chop to form a pocket. Mix the cottage cheese with the coriander and a pinch of salt and pepper. Use this to stuff the chops then press the slit together to seal the edges.

Mix the yoghurt with the garlic, lemon juice, cinnamon and paprika. Spread this over the chops, cover and leave in the refrigerator overnight.

Next day, lift the chops out of the dish and let most of the yoghurt mixture drip off. Dip each chop in flour, then beaten egg and finally in the breadcrumbs. Shallow fry the coated chops in hot oil for 5 minutes on each side.

Mild Pork

If you are giving a dinner party it is a good idea to include a mild dish like this one among your more fiery specialities. There is usually someone who will appreciate this consideration. This dish will also find favour with children and is a gentle introduction to Indian food.

¾ k (1½ lb) lean diced pork
2 tablespoons puréed papaya
1 onion
1 clove garlic, crushed
50 g (2 oz) ghee or butter
1 tablespoon oil
1 teaspoon dried mango powder
1 teaspoon ground cumin
1 clove
½ bay leaf
25 g (1 oz) creamed coconut
rind of 1 lemon, grated
50 g (2 oz) blanched almonds
pinch of salt
150 ml (¼ pint) plain yoghurt

Mix the pork with the papaya purée and leave to stand for 2 hours. Quarter the onion and separate out the layers.

Fry the onion and garlic in the ghee or butter and oil with the mango powder, cumin, clove and bay leaf. Add the meat and cook until the pork is sealed.

Melt the creamed coconut in 300 ml (½ pt) of hot water and add to the pan with the lemon rind, almonds and salt. Cover tightly and cook gently until the meat is tender.

Finally, stir in the yoghurt to give a creamy sauce and serve.

Sugared Pork Korma

This recipe is for a mild korma. The pork fillet absorbs flavour well and cooks fairly quickly. Try serving it with exotic spiced rice or parathas and a crisp vegetable dish such as cumin grated carrots.

juice of 1 lemon
¾ k (1½ lb) pork fillet, diced
150 ml (¼ pt) plain yoghurt
1 teaspoon garam masala
2 onions
50 g (2 oz) ghee or butter
pinch of paprika (or more if liked)
1 tsp turmeric
25 g (1 oz) creamed coconut
1 bay leaf
2 cloves
1 tablespoon soft brown sugar
3 tablespoons cream

Pour the lemon juice over the diced pork. Mix the yoghurt with the garam masala and stir this in with the meat. Cover and leave overnight in the refrigerator.

Next day cut the onions into quarters and separate out the layers. Fry these in the ghee or butter with the paprika, and turmeric for 3-4 minutes. Turn the heat up and add the meat. Cook briskly until the moisture has evaporated, then pour in 175 ml (6 fl oz) of water. Add the creamed coconut and stir until it has dissolved. Pop in the bay leaf and cloves, cover and cook gently for 45 minutes. Sprinkle the sugar over the meat and stir in the cream just before serving.

Vegetable Dishes

Many, many Indians are vegetarians. This partially stems from a scarcity of meat, but also has its roots in religion. The cow was particularly prized for its dairy produce and to kill a fertile cow was an economic sin long before it was proclaimed sacred. The high-caste Brahmins were especially fastidious and as they spread their religion southwards so they took with them the principles of vegetarianism. Northern India has been far more affected by foreign influences than the south and snatches of different cultures and cuisines can be seen there.

Vegetables have, therefore, been taken very seriously by Indian cooks and the tasty and imaginative dishes that are enjoyed today are the results of centuries of development.

Outside the major Indian cities freezers and even fridges are not common. Commercial freezing is also still in its infancy and canned foods tend to be expensive so virtually all foodstuffs are bought fresh. Every small town boasts a lively vegetable market where people from the surrounding area sell their produce. The displays are dazzling and the competition fierce.

In recent years our greengrocers and supermarkets have been stocking a wide range of exotic, imported vegetables. While India is not a major exporter of vegetables lots of these items are everyday fare there. Recipes in this section will help you to use some of these unusual products and turn them into curries, cutlets, fritters and main meals. Unlike meat, vegetables are rarely marinaded, but all the recipes do use spices to a greater or lesser degree.

When planning an Indian meal try to balance the textures as well as the flavours. Plenty of Indians eat all their food with their fingers, so meals have to be manageable. For example, rice is better at mopping up wet curries than chappaties or nan. If in doubt, follow some of the sample menus given.

Aubergines *(also known as brinjal and eggplant)*
Aubergines have dark purple skins and firm creamy coloured flesh containing numerous tiny, edible seeds. Buy them when the skin is shiny and taut. To prepare, wash and cut into good sized chunks (they shrink during cooking) then sprinkle with salt. Leave to stand for ½ hour then rinse well and pat dry. This removes the indigestible juices.

Courgettes *(also known as zucchini)*
These are not as common in India as the full-grown marrow. Courgettes have a stronger flavour but peeled, diced marrow is a perfectly adequate, and cheaper, substitute. Smaller young marrows with thinner skins may not need peeling but are still usually seeded before use. Because of their higher water content, marrow dishes need less liquid than their courgette counterparts.

Chillies *(also known as red peppers)*
This is a tropical plant and although not a native of Asia, India is now a major user and exporter of them. They vary in appearance and flavour from the fat, milder pods grown in East and West Africa to the long, thin fierce type found in India. They turn from green to red as they ripen. Good quality fat Kenyan chillies are available in many supermarkets but the Indian chillies are most easily obtainable from Asian or specialist shops.

Choose chillies that are not shrivelled up or discoloured. To prepare, wash and cut off the stalk end before slicing. The white seeds are the 'hottest' part and may be discarded. Contact with the skin, and in particular the eyes, can cause irritation so treat the chillies with respect. Wash hands after preparing them or wear rubber gloves. If Indian chillies are unavailable use dried red chillies.

Okra *(also known as lady's fingers and bhindi)*
It is important that you buy young, tender okra. Pods over 15 cm (6in) in length are likely to be tough and fibrous. The ribbed green pods contain fat, white edible seeds and a glutinous substance. To prevent the vegetable becoming slimy, wipe rather than wash and dry thoroughly before slicing, then cook immediately.

Pepper *(also known as capsicums and sweet or red or green peppers)*
High in vitamin C, these 'fruits' are both attractive and tasty. The peppers are red or yellow when ripe, but are commonly picked early and sold while still bright green. In general, the larger the pepper the milder its flavour. They can be eaten raw in salads or cooked. The cluster of white seeds is usually discarded.

Sweet Potatoes *(also known as yams)*
Sweet potatoes have a pinkish, purpley skin and creamy-coloured flesh. They can be treated like a potato and will boil, bake, mash or fry. They have a slightly higher sugar content than other tubers – hence the name – and are rather more filling.

Yams
These tropical root vegetables are usually larger and thicker than potatoes and have a thick, brown skin. Like sweet potatoes, they can be cooked as ordinary potatoes although they are not as nutritious. The flesh is either white or yellow depending on the variety.

Alu Bara Mirchi

Bara mirchi or sweet peppers are used widely in India. Alu is the Hindustani word for potato.

1 red, 1 green and 1 yellow sweet pepper
275 g (10 oz) potatoes, peeled and diced
450 ml (¾ pt) chicken or vegetable stock
25 g (1 oz) ghee or butter
3 tablespoons oil
2 onions, sliced
½ teaspoon paprika
25 g (1 oz) raisins
50 g (2 oz) skinned almonds
pinch of salt

Cut the capsicums in half lengthwise, remove the stalk and seeds and slice thinly. Parboil the potatoes in the stock.

Heat the ghee or butter and oil in a pan and fry the onions and capsicums for 5 minutes. Do not let them become too brown. Stir in the paprika, potatoes and 150 ml (¼ pt) of the stock. Cover and simmer until the potatoes are cooked.

Add the raisins, almonds and salt to the pan and cook gently until the raisins have plumped up and the liquid has evaporated.

Alu Bara Mirchi.

Stuffed Okra

There are two basic requirements for making stuffed okra. One is that the okra must be young and not blackened on the outside. The other is that you have the patience to stuff these fiddly little fingers. It is worth the effort and they make an attractive and tasty side dish.

275 g (10 oz) fresh, tender okra (lady's fingers)
50 g (2 oz) desiccated coconut
2 tablespoons lemon juice
25 g (1 oz) ghee or butter
oil
2 cloves garlic, crushed
1 onion, finely chopped
1 cm (½ in) piece fresh ginger, grated
1½ teaspoons turmeric
½ teaspoon paprika
2 teaspoons ground coriander

Bhindi Bhaji (left); Spiced Courgettes (right).

Wipe the okra with a damp cloth and dry thoroughly. Trim off the stalks and set aside. Put the coconut into a bowl and pour 150 ml (¼ pt) boiling water and the lemon juice over and leave to stand.

Heat the ghee or butter with 2 tablespoons of oil and fry the garlic, onion and ginger. Stir in the turmeric, paprika and coriander and fry for 1 minute. Drain the coconut, reserving the liquor, and add the flesh to the pan with a pinch of salt. Cook the mixture in the pan for 3 to 4 minutes then allow to cool.

Make a slit in each okra about 1 cm (½ in) joined at either end. Carefully force open the pod and stuff with the mixture. This is easier to do by hand than with a teaspoon. Press the filling in well.

Heat a couple of spoons of oil in a shallow lidded pan and lay in the stuffed okra. Cook for five minutes then pour over the coconut liquor, cover the pan and simmer very gently for 6 minutes.

Variation: As an alternative, beat 1 egg with 2 tablespoons milk and 1 tablespoon of flour to make a thin batter. Dip the okra into this and deep fry until crisp, about 4 minutes. Do not worry if some of the batter parts company with the okra.

Khumbar Mattar

This rich pea and mushroom dish has its origins in Kashmir, the northernmost state in India. Exotic morel mushrooms flourish happily in the woodlands above the vale of Kashmir. Substitute button or flat mushrooms if morels are not available.

275 g (10 oz) morel, flat or button mushrooms
2 onions
3 tablespoons oil
½ teaspoon black mustard seeds
2 teaspoons cumin seeds, dry roasted then ground
1 teaspoon turmeric
225 g (8 oz) peas, preferably fresh
3 dried red chillies
pinch of asafoetida (optional)
450 g (1 lb) ripe tomatoes, quartered and de-seeded
2½ teaspoons garam masala

Wash and dry the mushrooms and cut into quarters. Slice one onion finely. Roughly chop the other onion and liquidize until pulpy.

Heat the oil in a saucepan and fry the mustard seeds until they pop. Keep the pan covered until all sputtering noises stop. Add the ground cumin seeds, turmeric and the sliced onion. Cook uncovered until the onion starts to turn golden. Remove the mixture from the pan, but leave enough oil to coat the base.

Stir in the puréed onion and cook until it is thick and quite dry. To this add the peas, mushrooms, dried chillies, asafoetida, if using and tomatoes. Cover and cook gently until the peas are tender. Finally, mix in the spiced onion slices, garam masala and a seasoning of salt. If the mixture is dry pour in a little water. Cover tightly and simmer very gently for 15-20 minutes.

Bhindi Bhaji

Bhajis can be eaten on their own as a snack but also complement soft-textured dishes with their crispness. Bhajis make a useful adjunct to a vegetarian diet. Try substituting sliced onion or mushrooms.

3 spring onions, chopped
2 cloves garlic, crushed
125 g (5 oz) plain flour
250 ml (8 fl oz) milk
225 g (8 oz) fresh okra (also known as bhindi and lady's fingers)
1 egg plus 1 egg yolk, lightly beaten
1 pinch of salt
1 pinch of paprika
2 green chillies, finely sliced
oil for deep frying

Liquidize the spring onions, garlic and 1 tablespoon of the flour with 3 tablespoons of milk.

Wipe the okra, trim off the stalk end and slice into pieces approximately 1 cm (½ in) long. Do not wash the okra after it has been cut as it will exude a sticky liquid.

Sieve the remaining flour into a bowl. Combine the eggs with the remaining milk. Gradually work this into the flour to make a batter. Season with a pinch of salt and paprika and stir in the okra, onion paste and the sliced chillies.

Heat oil in a deep frying pan and when hot add a few heaped teaspoons of the mixture. Allow to brown all over, turning them occasionally. Remove and drain. Repeat until the mixture is used up. Serve while hot.

Coconut Curry

Coconut appears in many South Indian dishes and is considered an essential ingredient. With the abundant coconut palms found in the south, it is used freshly grated or infused in water to make coconut milk. Desiccated or creamed coconut can be substituted. It is a delicious accompaniment to mutton, chicken or vegetable curries.

1 fresh coconut, grated, or 225 g (8 oz) unsweetened desiccated coconut
2 cm (¾ in) piece of fresh ginger, peeled and chopped
2 cloves garlic
2 teaspoons chickpea flour (gram flour)
2 onions, sliced
3 tablespoons oil
½ teaspoon black mustard seeds
1 teaspoon ground cumin
1 teaspoon turmeric
2 fresh green chillies, sliced
25 g (1 oz) ghee or butter
25 g (1 oz) creamed coconut
2 carrots, grated
rind and juice of 1 lemon
100 g (4 oz) toasted flaked almonds

Soak the coconut in 250 ml (8 fl oz) of warm water for two hours. Liquidize the ginger, garlic, chickpea flour and half the onion to form a paste.

Heat the oil in a pan and add the mustard seeds when hot. Cook covered until they burst with a 'popping' noise. Stir in the cumin, turmeric, chillies and sliced onion and cook until the onion is soft but not brown. Stir in the liquidized paste with the butter and the creamed coconut. Lower the heat and continue to cook and stir for 3 minutes. Add the carrot, lemon juice and rind, coconut and the liquid to the pan. Stir well and cook uncovered until almost dry.

Serve on a platter garnished with the toasted almonds.

Spiced Courgettes

This easy way of preparing courgettes can be used for a variety of other vegetables. Try making it with shredded cabbage, sliced parsnips or carrots, diced sweet potatoes or fresh green beans. There is a recipe for home-made curry powder on page 11, but if you use ready-mixed powder, make sure it is fresh.

450 g (1 lb) courgettes
4 tablespoons oil
1 onion, sliced
1 cm (½ in) piece of fresh ginger, grated
1 level teaspoon curry powder
3 large tomatoes, peeled and quartered
150 ml (¼ pt) water
salt and pepper

Wash the courgettes and cut off the ends. Slice them in four lengthwise and then into 5 cm (2 in) sticks.

Heat the oil in a large, lidded frying pan. Stir-fry the onion and courgettes over a fairly high heat until the courgettes have browned all over. Add the ginger and the curry powder and cook for 1 minute.

Add the tomato pieces, water and a generous amount of salt and pepper. Mix all the ingredients together, lower the heat, cover the pan tightly and simmer for 12 minutes.

Remove the lid and cook for a minute to reduce the sauce slightly. Serve with thick vegetable dhal and pullau rice or a dry meat dish.

Potato and Bean Foogath

The difference between this recipe and that for carrot foogath is that this calls for the main ingredients to be pre-cooked. Follow this recipe, varying it with any vegetable which takes a long time to cook or as a good way to use up left-overs. Cumin is used here to complement the potato but can be omitted if using other vegetables.

4 tablespoons oil
2 onions, sliced
3 cloves garlic, crushed
3 fresh chillies, sliced or 1 teaspoon chilli powder
2 teaspoons whole cumin seeds
15 g (½ oz) ghee or butter
25 g (1 oz) creamed coconut
225 g (8 oz) cooked or tinned red kidney beans
225 g (8 oz) cooked, diced potatoes
pinch of salt
15 g (½ oz) unsweetened desiccated coconut

Heat the oil in a frying pan and cook the onions until soft. Stir in the garlic, chillies and the cumin seeds and cook for 2 minutes.

Add the ghee or butter and creamed coconut to the pan and when melted mix in the beans, potatoes, salt and desiccated coconut.

Gently stir the foogath to make sure it is thoroughly combined, but try not to break up the potatoes. Continue to cook for 8-10 minutes adding small quantities of water if the mixture starts to stick to the pan. The end result should be quite dry and very tasty.

Yellow Cabbage

This mild South Indian dish is quick and easy to prepare. It makes an excellent supper and is delicious served with very spicy meat dishes or as part of a vegetarian meal.

1 tablespoon oil
1 teaspoon black mustard seeds
1 teaspoon turmeric
3 onions, sliced
350 g (12 oz) hard white cabbage, sliced
175 ml (6 fl oz) vegetable stock
¼ teaspoon salt
2 tablespoons grated fresh coconut or unsweetened desiccated coconut

Slice the onions and cabbage fairly finely and set to one side. Using a heavy-based pan with a lid, heat the oil until hot but not smoking. Scatter in the mustard seeds, replace the lid and cook over a moderate heat until the seeds pop. When the sputtering stops add the turmeric and cook for 30 seconds.

Stir in the sliced onions and cabbage, taking care to coat them thoroughly with the oil and spices. Replace the lid and sweat over a low heat for 5 minutes.

Pour in 125 ml (4 fl oz) of the stock, the salt and the coconut. Stir again and cover tightly. Cook over a low heat for 6 minutes. The liquid should be absorbed by the mixture and the cabbage should still be slightly crunchy. If the cabbage is tough add the remaining stock and cook until tender. Any excess liquid can be evaporated quickly by turning up the heat and removing the lid.

Carrot Foogath

Foogath is a name which covers a multitude of vegetable dishes. Similar preparations will also appear all over India under different names. Basically they are simple, quick side dishes with one foundation and into which almost any vegetable can be added.

30 ml (1 fl oz) oil
2 onions, sliced
3 cloves garlic, crushed
3 fresh chillies, sliced or 1 teaspoon chilli powder
1 cm (½ in) piece of fresh ginger, peeled and grated
25 g (1 oz) creamed coconut
350 g (12 oz) carrots, grated

Heat the oil in a frying pan and cook the onions until soft. Add the garlic, chillies and ginger and continue to fry for 2 minutes.

Stir in the creamed coconut with the grated carrot. If the mixture sticks to the bottom of the pan add 15 ml (½ fl oz) of water and mix well. Keep stirring and adding small amounts of water if necessary until the carrot is just soft. Season with a pinch of salt.

Potato and Bean Foogath (left); Carrot Foogath (right); Yellow Cabbage (bottom).

Spinach Koftas

Spinach Koftas are deep fried to give a crisp shell with a delicious soft centre. They make an attractive addition to any meal or can be eaten as a snack dipped into coconut chutney.

350 g (12 oz) fresh spinach
2 green chillies, chopped
50 g (2 oz) chickpea flour (gram flour)
225 g (8 oz) (½ tin) cooked chickpeas
½ teaspoon ground cardamom seeds
pinch of all-spice
salt and pepper
oil for deep frying

Wash the spinach thoroughly and cook in 4 tablespoons of water until tender. Drain and press in a sieve to remove all moisture.

Place the spinach with all the other ingredients except the oil in a liquidizer or food processor and work until you have a thick bright green paste.

Heat the oil in a deep-fat pan and when hot drop in teaspoons of the paste. Fry the koftas for 2-3 minutes or until the outsides are crisp and starting to turn golden. Remove with a slotted spoon and keep warm in the oven. Do not try to cook too many at one time, and take care not to break them while they are in the oil.

Serve as soon as they are all cooked.

Yam Koftas

If the brown yams are not available, pink-skinned sweet potatoes can be substituted in this recipe. A favourite way of eating these koftas is to pop them into a pan of simple courgette curry, to absorb some more flavour. Let them simmer very gently in the curry for 15 minutes then serve with yellow rice and a dry dish such as brinjal cutlets or tandoori chicken.

1 large yam (approximately 350 g or 12 oz), peeled
225 g (8oz) potatoes, peeled
2 green chillies, finely chopped
25 g (1 oz) plain flour
½ teaspoon ground cardamom seeds
1 teaspoon salt
1 tablespoon desiccated coconut
1 clove garlic, crushed
¼ teaspoon grated nutmeg
oil for deep frying

Boil the yam and the potatoes until they are cooked. Drain and return to the pan over the heat, shaking them until they are dry, then mash them.

Combine all the ingredients except the oil and mix thoroughly.

Dust your hands with flour and form balls with the mixture, taking about 1 tablespoon of it for each ball. Chill for ½ hour.

Heat the oil in a deep frying pan and when hot slide in a few koftas. Turn them gently and cook for about 3 minutes. Keep the cooked koftas warm in the oven while cooking the rest.

Vegetable Layer Bake

This unusual recipe has been included to show the results of imaginative cooking. It was invented by an Anglo-Indian friend in England and makes a marvellous main dish for a vegetarian meal. Serve with moist pullau rice, bhajis and spicy mango chutney.

2 aubergines
30 ml (1 fl oz) oil
2 teaspoons cumin seeds
2 cloves garlic, crushed
225 g (8 oz) cooked, diced potatoes
1 tablespoon desiccated coconut
2 tablespoons mango chutney
lime pickle to taste, chopped
175 g (6 oz) tomatoes, sliced
salt and pepper
300 ml (½ pt) thick yoghurt
fresh coriander leaves to garnish

Slice the aubergine thinly. Sprinkle with salt and leave for 10 minutes, then rinse and dry.

Heat half the oil in a shallow pan and fry the cumin seeds with the garlic. Stir in the potato dice and coconut and cook until golden brown. Place in the bottom of a large ovenproof dish. Dab the surface with 2 tablespoons of mango chutney. Heat the remaining oil and fry the aubergines a few at a time, until crisp. Drain and arrange on top of the potato and mango.

Spread the lime pickle over the aubergines.

Slice the tomatoes, season with a little salt and pepper and lay these on top.

Finally, spoon the thick yoghurt over and bake, uncovered, in a medium oven for 20 minutes. Garnish with whole coriander leaves.

Beans in Akni

Beans in Akni (left); Mushroom Stuffed Cabbage Leaves (right).

Akni is the name given to a light vegetable and spice stock or court bouillon. There are many different combinations of flavourings which are acceptable. This version marries well with lots of vegetables, so try using it for steamed or boiled potatoes, root vegetables or even asparagus. Serve the cooked beans with a rich meat dish like roghan josh and pullau rice.

225 g (8 oz) fresh runner beans
225 g (8 oz) fresh French beans
1 onion
1 teaspoon mustard seeds
2 teaspoons coriander seeds
3 bay leaves
1 clove garlic
1 cm (½ in) fresh ginger
225 g (8 oz) fresh or frozen broad beans, shelled
50 g (2 oz) ghee or butter
sprig of fresh thyme
salt and pepper

Slice the runner beans diagonally into thin strips. Top and tail the French beans.

Chop the onion finely. Lightly crush the mustard and coriander seeds and crumble the bay leaves. Peel the garlic and bruise it. Peel the ginger and grate coarsely. Combine all these aromatics in a piece of muslin and tie up to make a 'bouquet garni'. Place this in a large pan with about 1 litre (2 pts) of cold water. Bring to the boil slowly and then simmer gently for about 30 minutes. Remove the spices from the pan.

Add the broad beans and cook for 5 minutes then add the other beans and continue to simmer for a further 4 minutes. Drain off the akni and reserve.

Melt the ghee or butter with the sprig of thyme. Allow this to heat slowly for 2-3 minutes. When hot and starting to foam stir in all the drained beans. Season with salt and pepper and toss thoroughly. Serve immediately.

The reserved akni can be strained through muslin to remove any bits of bean, cooled and stored in covered jars in the fridge for further use. Do not keep for more than 4-5 days.

Alu Sukke

Alu Sukke (dry spiced potato) can be eaten as an accompaniment to a main meal or served as a snack in delicious chickpea pancakes. Choose floury potatoes rather than the waxy type as these will absorb the flavours better.

450 g (1 lb) floury potatoes
5 tablespoons oil
¼ teaspoon mustard seeds
¼ teaspoon fennel seeds
½ teaspoon turmeric
1 teaspoon ground cumin
1 teaspoon ground coriander
2 teaspoons sesame seeds
2 onions, chopped
3 fresh green chillies, sliced
1 cm (½ in) piece of fresh ginger, grated
2 teaspoons mango chutney
150 ml (¼ pint) water
25 g (1 oz) creamed coconut
pinch of salt
3 tomatoes, quartered

Parboil the potatoes, peel and cut into small dice.

Heat the oil in a large, lidded frying pan and cook the mustard and fennel seeds until they pop. Stir in the turmeric, cumin, coriander and sesame seeds and continue to cook for 1 minute.

Add the chopped onion with the chillies and ginger, stirring well to prevent anything sticking to the pan. At this stage the mixture should be quite oily. Slide the potato dice into the pan and stir to mix well with the spices. Cook until the potatoes begin to brown on the outside.

Mix the mango chutney with 150 ml (¼ pt) of hot water, the creamed coconut and salt. Pour this into the pan and add the tomatoes. Lower the heat, cover the pan and simmer very gently for 20 minutes, stirring occasionally.

Remove the lid and cook uncovered, stirring all the time until all the liquid has evaporated and you are left with rich sticky potato dice. Take care not to mash the potatoes during this final stage.

Peanut Potato Rissoles

These are eaten as a snack in India, although they could accompany a meal. In the northern states they are sold on street corners and dipped into green or coconut chutney. Try these crunchy potato rissoles with Tandoori Chicken and fresh salad.

450 g (1 lb) old potatoes
4 tablespoons oil
10 fenugreek seeds
1 teaspoon ground cumin
2 teaspoons ground coriander
1 onion, finely chopped
2 green chillies, finely sliced
50 g (2 oz) cooked or tinned chickpeas, chopped
50 g (2 oz) peanuts, chopped
2.5 cm (1 in) piece fresh ginger, peeled and grated
2 tablespoons lemon juice
1 small bunch fresh coriander leaves, chopped

Peel the potatoes, boil until tender in lightly salted water, drain and mash.

Heat 2 tablespoons of oil in a shallow pan and when hot fry the fenugreek seeds with the ground cumin and coriander for 1 minute. Add the chopped onion and chillies and stir over a medium heat until softened. Mix in the chickpeas, peanuts, grated ginger and lemon juice. Continue to cook, stirring occasionally, until thick and sticky. Add the coriander leaves to the mixture then allow to cool.

Form balls with the mashed potato, using your hands. This amount will make about 10. Slice each ball in half and spoon some of the peanut mixture onto one half of each ball. Reassemble the potato cakes, pressing the tops on firmly to make neat flat rissoles. Chill for ½ hour in the refrigerator.

Heat 2 tablespoons of the oil in a wide shallow pan and fry the rissoles, allowing to brown on one side before turning them carefully. As soon as they are golden brown they are ready to eat.

Mushroom Stuffed Cabbage Leaves

There are lots of recipes for different stuffings for cabbage leaves and everyone has their favourite. This one incorporates cooked pulses and gives a good firm parcel. Try inventing your own filling based, perhaps, on another vegetable dish or even a spiced minced meat recipe like kheema. Serve them warm with your favourite rice recipe dish and one other vegetable dish.

1 green cabbage
50 g (2 oz) split red lentils
3 tablespoons oil
15 g (½ oz) ghee or butter
½ teaspoon mustard seeds
1 onion, finely chopped
350 g (12 oz) mushrooms, finely chopped
2 teaspoons ground coriander
1 teaspoon turmeric
salt and pepper

Bring a large pan of water to the boil and slide in the whole cabbage. Boil for 5 minutes, remove from the pan and plunge it into cold water. Keep the cabbage water.

Carefully begin to remove the outer leaves from the cabbage. Place them to dry on kitchen paper. The inner leaves will still be quite crisp and difficult to remove so place the cabbage back into the pan and boil for a few more minutes. When you have 12-14 good leaves stop and chop the remaining cabbage finely.

Meanwhile, wash the lentils and cover with cold water, bring to the boil and cook until very soft. A tablespoon of oil in the water will prevent a thick scum forming. Drain the lentils and set on one side.

Heat the oil and ghee or butter in a pan and cook the mustard seeds until they pop. Add the chopped onion and mushrooms and stir-fry over a high heat for 3 minutes. Remove from the pan with a slotted spoon. Now stir in the ground coriander, turmeric and chopped cabbage. Fry for 3 minutes then pour 4 tablespoons of the cabbage water over. Cover tightly and cook until the cabbage is just tender. Take off the lid and stir in the cooked lentils, onions and mushrooms. Stir until all the liquid has evaporated. Season with salt and pepper and allow to cool.

Take each cabbage leaf and place a tablespoon of the stuffing in the centre. Tuck two sides in then roll to form neat parcels. It may be necessary to snip out the tough stalk from the outer leaves. Do this with a pair of scissors, but try to keep the leaf intact.

Place the cabbage rolls in a casserole dish and pour over 125 ml (4 fl oz) of the cabbage water. Cover and bake for 25 minutes at Gas Mark 4, 180°C, 360°F.

Drain off the liquid and return uncovered to the oven for 5 minutes to dry.

Brinjal Cutlets

To make these cutlets choose short plump aubergines that still have the stalk attached. These make an ideal main dish for a vegetarian meal and are delicious served with dhal and khumbar mattar.

2/3 aubergines (also known as brinjal and eggplants)
2 onions, chopped
4 cloves garlic, crushed
4 green chillies, sliced
2.5 cm (1 in) piece fresh ginger, peeled and grated
1 large carrot, grated
50 g (2 oz) long grain rice
1 teaspoon turmeric
30 ml (1 fl oz) oil
¼ teaspoon salt
1 egg, beaten
75 g (3 oz) dried breadcrumbs

Slice the aubergines in half lengthwise splitting the stalk in two. Scoop out most of the flesh leaving just a thin layer inside the skin. Plunge the shells into salted boiling water and cook for 3 minutes. Drain and set aside on kitchen paper to dry.

Chop the scooped out aubergine flesh and combine with the onion, garlic, chillies, ginger and carrot.

Cook the rice in boiling water with the turmeric until tender. Drain.

Heat 3 tablespoons of the oil in a shallow pan and fry the vegetable mixture for 5 minutes, stirring all the time. Mix in the salt and cooked rice. Spoon the mixture into the aubergine shells and press well with the back of a spoon. Allow to cool completely.

Coat the cutlets first in egg and then in breadcrumbs.

Heat the remaining oil in a large frying pan and carefully slide the cutlets into the hot fat. Cook for 3 minutes over a medium heat then turn the cutlets over and continue to cook until brown and crisp.

Brinjal Boortha

Brinjal Boortha may be served hot with a pullau dish or cold almost like a dip with puris or chappaties. It should have a rich creamy texture and an irresistible taste. It includes raw garlic, so serve sprigs of fresh parsley and roasted fennel seeds as a breath freshener.

2 medium aubergines (brinjal or eggplants)
2 spring onions, chopped
1 fresh chilli, chopped
25 g (1 oz) desiccated coconut
2 cloves garlic, crushed
juice and rind of 1 lemon
½ teaspoon salt
3 tablespoons olive oil

Wash the aubergines and leave whole. Place them on a baking tray and bake them in a hot oven for ½ hour or until soft, turning occasionally. The skin will char during this time and give off a delicious aroma. When the aubergine feels very soft, peel away the blackened skin. Liquidize the flesh with all the other ingredients except the oil. When thoroughly combined slowly pour in the oil and mix well.

To make this dish without a liquidizer or food processor, mash all the ingredients very well with a fork then beat in the oil.

To serve hot, put the boortha in an ovenproof dish, cover tightly and bake in a medium oven for 15 minutes. Stir well before transferring to a serving dish.

South Indian-style Brinjal

Traditionally this dish would be served in small bowls (nowadays made of stainless steel) as part of a 'Thali'. A Thali would include a selection of wet and dry spicy vegetables, a heap of perfectly cooked rice, a stack of delicate puris, some hot pickle and a raita.

350 g (12 oz) aubergines (brinjal or eggplant)
4 spring onions
397 g (14 oz) can of tomatoes or 5 large tomatoes
2 cloves garlic, crushed
3 tablespoons oil
25 g (1 oz) ghee or butter
2.5 cm (1 in) piece of fresh ginger, grated
2 teaspoons ground coriander
2 small dried red chillies, finely chopped
2 tablespoons fresh, chopped coriander leaves
salt

Cut the aubergines into 2.5 cm (1 in) chunks, place on a plate and sprinkle with salt. Leave for 15 minutes then rinse and drain. This draws out the indigestible juices.

Trim the spring onions down to about 6 cm (2 in) then slice into quarters lengthwise. Roughly chop the tinned tomatoes or quarter the fresh tomatoes.

Put the garlic into a pan with ¾ l (1 ½ pints) of water and bring to the boil. Add the chunks of aubergine and boil for 4 minutes. Drain and dry on kitchen paper.

Heat the oil and fry the soft aubergine pieces until they begin to brown and give off a nutty aroma. Remove from the pan with a slotted spoon. Add the ghee or butter to the pan and allow it to begin to bubble, then fry the ginger, spring onion, ground coriander and chillies for 1 minute. Finally stir in the tomatoes with the aubergines and chopped coriander leaves. Season with salt, lower the heat and simmer gently for 5 minutes. Allow to cool slightly before eating.

Cumin Grated Carrot

This dish is very quick and simple to make. The carrots should still have a slight 'bite' to them after cooking so if you are serving this at a dinner party, assemble all the prepared ingredients and then cook them at the last minute. The raisins are not traditional, but taste good and are worth trying. Parsnips can be added or even used instead of the carrots.

5 tablespoons oil
2 onions, chopped
3 cloves garlic, crushed
3 teaspoons cumin seeds, dry roasted and ground
225 g (8 oz) carrots, grated
2 tablespoons raisins
rind and juice of 1 orange
salt and pepper

Heat the oil in a frying pan and cook the onion with the garlic until just starting to brown. Add the cumin and carrots and stir-fry for 3 minutes.

Stir in the raisins, rind and juice of the orange and season with salt and pepper. Continue to cook for 3 minutes over a medium heat. Serve immediately.

Cumin Grated Carrot.

Tomato and Fenugreek Pitla

Tomatoes play an important part in cooking all over India. This rather unusual green tomato dish comes from central India and is eaten with crispy golden puris.

1 onion, chopped
2 teaspoons chickpea flour (gram flour)
125 ml (¼ pt) water
3 tablespoons oil
½ teaspoon black mustard seeds
1 teaspoon cumin seeds
6 fenugreek seeds
1 teaspoon turmeric
675 g (1½ lb) green tomatoes, quartered
3 green chillies, finely sliced
pinch of salt
fresh coriander to garnish

Liquidize the onion with the chickpea flour and water to make a thin paste.

Heat the oil in a shallow lidded pan and when hot add the mustard, cumin and fenugreek seeds. Cover and cook until the seeds burst with a popping noise. Stir in the turmeric, tomatoes and chillies and fry for 3 minutes.

Add the onion paste and stir over a gentle heat until the mixture begins to simmer and thicken. Replace the lid and cook for a further 5 minutes. Season with salt and serve garnished with coriander leaves.

Paneer Mattar

Paneer is similar to cottage cheese and is used in both savoury and sweet dishes. Try it with yellow rice and a spicy fish dish.

Paneer
Bring ½l (1 pint) of milk to the boil and stir in the juice of 1 lemon. Cook until the milk curdles then strain through a clean piece of muslin. Leave overnight to drip through and do not be tempted to squeeze it. Next day the ball of cheese will be ready to use.

walnut-sized piece of tamarind soaked in 150 ml (¼ pt) warm water
*   overnight or 150 ml (¼ pt) vegetable stock*
25 g (1 oz) ghee or butter
1 tablespoon oil
¼ teaspoon fenugreek seeds
2 teaspoons ground coriander
1 teaspoon turmeric
2 onions, sliced
2 fresh chillies, sliced
275 g (10 oz) fresh or frozen peas
pinch of salt
100 g (4 oz) paneer or thick cottage cheese

Strain the tamarind liquid through a sieve pushing the pulpy flesh through and discarding any hard bits. Reserve the pulpy liquid.

Heat the ghee or butter and oil in a saucepan and fry the fenugreek seeds, coriander and turmeric for 1 minute.

Add the onions and chillies and cook gently until softened. Stir in the peas and 150 ml (¼ pt) of either tamarind water or vegetable stock. Simmer until the peas are tender and the liquid has evaporated. Season with a pinch of salt and carefully fold in the paneer or cottage cheese just before serving.

Madras-style Mixed Vegetables

Madras food has gained notoriety for being extremely hot. Of course this is an over-simplification as there are many styles of cooking found in the Madras district, but in any case this searing heat is not truly essential. If you do not like hot food simply follow the recipe but reduce the amount of chillies or chilli powder, or even do away with it altogether. The result will be different but no less delicious. Remember that a yoghurt-based raita or chutney will take the sting out of highly spiced food.

100 g (4 oz) green beans
275 g (10 oz) potatoes, diced
½ fresh coconut or 25 g (1 oz) creamed coconut
50 g (2 oz) ghee or butter
2 tablespoons oil
3 onions, chopped
4 cloves garlic, crushed
1 teaspoon ground coriander
½ teaspoon turmeric
3-5 dried red chillies or 1-2 teaspoons chilli powder
6 tomatoes, quartered
1 aubergine (brinjal or eggplant), diced
½ teaspoon salt

Paneer Mattar (left); Madras-style Mixed Vegetable (right).

Cut the beans into 2.5 cm (1 in) lengths. Parboil the potatoes for 4 minutes then drain and set aside.

Grate the flesh of the coconut and cover with 300 ml (½ pint) of boiling water. Allow to stand for 20 minutes then strain off the infused liquid. If using creamed coconut, mix with 300 ml (½ pint) boiling water and stir until it has dissolved.

Heat the ghee or butter and oil in a large pan. Fry the onion with the garlic, ground coriander and turmeric. Add the dried chillies or the powder and stir well.

Add all the vegetables and stir-fry for 4 minutes. As the tomatoes soften add the coconut liquid with the salt. Cover tightly and simmer gently for 20 minutes. Remove the lid and allow to cook for another 5 minutes to reduce the liquid by about half.

Serve as a main dish with chappaties or rice and chutneys and pickles.

Spiced Cauliflower

This method of cooking cauliflower renders it quite soft and would, no doubt, be out of favour with the 'al dente' band of cooks. However, only by slow simmering do the spices fully impregnate the vegetable. Eat it with crisp puris or chicken biriani and raita.

1 cauliflower
4 tablespoons oil
1 teaspoon mustard seeds
2 teaspoons ground cumin
1 teaspoon ground coriander
1 teaspoon turmeric
1 large onion, finely chopped
2 fresh chillies, finely chopped
3 cloves of garlic, crushed
397 g (14 oz) can of tomatoes, roughly chopped
1½ tablespoons chopped fresh coriander leaves
1 tablespoon tomato purée
1 teaspoon garam masala

Wash the cauliflower and divide it into small florets.

Heat the oil in a lidded pan and cook the mustard seeds until they pop. Stir in the ground cumin, ground coriander and turmeric and fry for 1 minute. Add the onion, chillies and garlic and continue to stir-fry until they begin to brown.

Take the cauliflower sprigs and add them to the pan, stirring well to coat them with the spices. Next add the tinned tomatoes, salt and fresh coriander.

Bring the mixture to the boil, then immediately reduce the heat, cover and simmer very gently for 10 minutes.

Combine the tomato purée with 150 ml (¼ pt) of boiling water. Gently stir this into the pan and sprinkle in the garam masala.

With the lid off the pan continue to cook until almost all the liquid has evaporated. The spiced cauliflower will need to be stirred towards the end of this process, but care must be taken not to mash everything to a pulp.

Grains and Pulses

Rice is the staple food of much of Asia and in India it is eaten in huge quantities with almost every meal. There are many different types of rice, of which the long-grained variety is the most popular. The more expensive basmati rice is considered to be the best. It is grown at the foot of the Himalayas and has attractive long, slim grains. Long-grain 'supermarket' rice will suffice for most of the recipes in this section, but I suggest you use basmati for special pullau and biriani dishes.

It is always wise to wash rice before cooking it. This removes any dust and some of the starch, thus preventing the rice becoming sticky. Soaking the rice beforehand helps to give brilliant white grains, which is highly regarded in India. If you prefer brown, unpolished rice simply follow the recipe but add half as much liquid again and cook until the rice is done.

In the northern states wheat also plays an important role in diet. Traditional Indian breads are usually round and flat in appearance. Many of them, like chappaties and parathas, are unleavened but the delicious nan uses yeast and yoghurt to produce a softer bread. Nan should be cooked by slapping rounds of the dough onto the inside of the clay tandoor oven, a domestic stove also gives good results.

Similarly chappaties would normally be rolled out into shape using a special round board, called a chakla, and a slim rolling pin tapered at each end. They are then cooked on a tawa, a heavy cast-iron plate.

Pulses are a good source of protein and roughage and when combined with dairy produce, nuts and cereal provide a healthy base for vegetarian diets. Vegetable dhal with rice and yoghurt is the sort of meal on which many peasants depend.

Pulses should be washed well before use. Soaking them reduces cooking time and makes them more digestible.

Most simple dhal dishes can be served thin and soup-like or cooked until firm and almost dry.

Chappaties

The dough is a simple mix of flour and water, but some experience is needed to turn out really good chappaties.

100 g (4 oz) plain flour
100 g (4 oz) wholewheat flour
pinch of salt
approximately 210 ml (7 fl oz) water
oil for shallow frying (optional)

Sieve the flours and salt into a bowl and gradually add enough water to make a firm yet pliable dough. The amount of water will vary according to the quality of flours used.

Knead the dough for 5 minutes on a lightly floured board then cover with cling wrap and chill for 2-3 hours.

Knead the dough again and divide into 10 equal-sized pieces. Knead each piece into a smooth ball and roll out to form rounds of about 15 cm (6 in), keeping the board and rolling pin well floured to prevent the dough from sticking.

For softer, floury chappaties heat a heavy-based frying pan or griddle and cook them 'dry'. Heating a small amount of oil in the pan gives the chappaties a rather more crisp outside.

In either case, cook the chappaties for about ½ minute on each side, then take each one with a pair of tongs and lay directly onto a gas flame or under a hot grill for a few seconds, which will puff them up.

Nan

This is a popular type of leavened bread, much softer than chappaties and very filling. I love making these as the dough is so pliable and silky it is a joy to work with. If the nans are to accompany a hearty main meal you may wish to make each one half its usual size.

150 ml (¼ pt) milk
21 g (¾ oz) fresh yeast or 1½ teaspoons dried yeast
1 teaspoon sugar
1 egg
3 dessertspoons plain yoghurt
25 g (1 oz) butter
400 g (14 oz) plain flour
1 teaspoon bicarbonate of soda
pinch of salt
1 tablespoon oil
3 teaspoons sesame seeds

Heat the milk until just lukewarm. Mix the yeast with the sugar and pour the warmed milk over. Set on one side for 10 minutes or until the mixture has a good head of froth.

Combine the egg with the yoghurt and stir into the yeasty milk. Melt the butter and add to the mixture.

Sieve the flour into a large bowl with the bicarbonate of soda and a good pinch of salt. Pour the mixture into the bowl and stir until all the flour is mixed in and you have a soft dough. Knead on a floured surface for 5-10 minutes until the dough is very smooth and silky. Place in an oiled bowl and cover with clingfilm. Leave to rise until doubled in size, about 1½ hours.

Set the oven to its maximum heat with the racks towards the top of the oven. Oil 2 large baking trays and put these into the hot oven.

Divide the risen dough into 5 equal pieces and knead each one into a smooth ball. Take one ball at a time and pull it out until you have an oval shape about 25 cm (10 in) long and 12 cm (5 in) wide. It is quite springy and you must treat the dough firmly. If you have a lot of trouble you can resort to a rolling pin.

When you have 4 nan prepared brush them on one side with a little milk or water and sprinkle with sesame seeds. Lay these onto the hot baking trays and cook for 3-4 minutes on each side. They should be pale gold in colour and still very soft inside.

Shape the last piece of dough and cook this as soon as you have space on the baking trays.

When cooked, wrap in foil and keep in a low oven until required. Nan freezes quite well. Individually wrap in foil. Reheat in a medium oven for about 15 minutes. Keep the foil on as this will prevent them from drying out and becoming hard.

Chappaties (left); Nan (bottom).

Parathas

The preparation time for making Parathas is quite
short, but the dough improves if it is allowed to 'rest' for an
hour or two. The end result is a crisp, butter bread which can
be eaten with almost all Indian dishes.

225 g (8 oz) plain flour
pinch of salt
100 g (2 oz) butter
approximately 175 ml (6 fl oz) water
oil for frying

Sieve the flour and salt into a bowl and rub in half of the butter lightly
with your fingers. Gradually work in enough water to produce a soft,
pliable dough. Knead the dough on a floured surface for 5 minutes
then cover with cling wrap and chill for 1-2 hours.

Melt the remaining butter. Divide the dough into 8 equal pieces
and knead each one into a smooth ball. Roll them out to form thin
rounds about 12 cm (6 in) across. Brush with melted butter and fold in
half. Brush with a little more butter and fold in half again to form a
triangle. Roll each triangle out again to form a circle and repeat the
process, so that you have built up lots of layers of dough and butter.
Take each triangle and roll it lightly until the sides are about 12 cm
(6 in) long.

Heat a little oil in a heavy-based frying pan or griddle and cook
the parathas over a gentle heat until they are brown on both sides. If
you have any melted butter left over brush this onto the parathas as
they are cooking.

Keema Stuffed Parathas

**Here a dry, spiced minced beef mixture is sandwiched between
layers of paratha dough and then fried. You can take this idea
and substitute any left-over dry meat or vegetable curries for
the keema. Serve Keema Stuffed Parathas with rice, dhal and
yoghurt for a tasty lunch.**

1 onion, chopped
1 dried red chilli, chopped
175 g (6 oz) minced beef
2 tablespoons oil
1 teaspoon grated fresh ginger
1 teaspoon garam masala
pinch of salt
225 g (8 oz) paratha dough (see above)
50 g (2 oz) butter, melted
oil for frying

To make the keema stuffing, fry the onion, chilli and minced beef in
the oil. When the beef is nicely brown stir in the ginger, garam masala
and 150 ml (¼ pt) of water. Season with a pinch of salt and simmer for
15-20 minutes. Cook quickly over a high heat to drive off any moisture, then allow the mixture to cool completely.

Take the paratha dough and divide it into 16 small balls. Press
each one on a floured board to flatten it, then roll out into 5 cm (2 in)
rounds. Brush them with melted butter and pair them off, putting the
buttered sides together. Roll each of these out to form rounds about
15 cm (6 in) across.

Spread half of the rounds with a little of the keema, leaving 1 cm
(½ in) clear around the edge. Brush the edge with water and place
another circle of dough on top. Roll them very carefully together
making sure that the edges are sealed.

Heat a little oil in a shallow pan and fry each stuffed paratha
slowly until golden brown on both sides.

Puris

**Puris can be served with any main meal, they should be very
light and crisp but not hard.**

50 g (2 oz) plain flour
50 g (2 oz) wholewheat flour
pinch of salt
10 g (½ oz) butter
2 teaspoons oil
water
oil for deep frying

Sieve the flours and salt together and rub in the butter. Pour in the oil
and rub in with your fingertips. Using cold water, pour in just
sufficient to make a pliable dough. Knead well for 5 minutes then
wrap in cling film and set aside for at least ¾ hour.

Divide the dough into 6 and knead each piece separately. Roll the
balls out on a floured surface until very thin. Slip one into very hot fat
in a deep fat fryer. Only cook one at a time and hold the puri under the
hot oil for 10-15 seconds or until it starts to puff up. Turn it over and
cook for a further 15-30 seconds. It should swell up and turn pale
golden in colour. Remove and keep in a warm oven until you have
finished the batch, then serve immediately.

If you have trouble rolling out the dough thinly enough, try
putting the ball of dough between two sheets of polythene or silicone
paper and then rolling it out.

Vegetable Dhal

This combination of pulses and vegetables is nutritious and forms an important part of the diet of many vegetarian Indians. This recipe is a basic one from South India but try experimenting with your favourite vegetables and mix of spices. There are no definitive recipes for dishes like this because vegetables vary according to season and what is grown locally. The dhal should be quite thick and would normally be served with plain rice or chappaties, pickles and poppadums. It can also be used as an accompaniment to a main meat dish.

275 g (10 oz) split red lentils (masoor dhal)
2 medium potatoes
3 carrots
2 courgettes
2 onions, chopped
2 cloves garlic, crushed
1 tablespoon grated fresh ginger
4 tablespoons oil
1½ teaspoons black mustard seeds
1 teaspoon ground cumin
1½ teaspoons turmeric
2 teaspoons ground coriander
2-3 dried red chillies, chopped
salt to taste

Wash the lentils and pick out any pieces of grit. Leave to stand in clean cold water for ½ hour.

Wash the potatoes, carrots and courgettes, peel if preferred, and cut into chunks or thick slices.

Gently fry the onions with the garlic and ginger in the oil until the onion begins to turn golden. Stir in the mustard seeds, cumin, turmeric, coriander and chillies and fry for a couple of minutes. Drain the lentils and add them to the pan. Mix thoroughly, then stir in the vegetable pieces. Season with salt and pour over ½ l (1 pt) of boiling water.

Bring to the boil and stir to loosen any bits that may be sticking to the base of the pan. Cover and simmer gently for about half an hour or until the vegetables are tender. Check the pan from time to time, adding more water when necessary.

When ready, the lentils will be very soft and thick but the vegetables should not be mushy.

Parathas (left) ; Puris (centre) ; Vegetable Dhal (right).

Toovar Dhal

Toovar dhal resembles the more familiar yellow split pea although it is a little larger. Split peas may be used in place of the toovar dhal. Serve this with plain rice and some pickles or chutneys for a simple lunch.

225 g (8 oz) toovar dhal, soaked for 12 hours
2 onions, sliced
2 cloves garlic, crushed
4 tablespoons oil
2 teaspoons home-made curry powder
1 dessertspoon grated fresh ginger
juice of 1 lime
2 pieces cassia or a small piece of cinnamon
salt
1 tablespoon chopped coriander leaves
3 hard-boiled eggs, sliced (optional)

Rinse the dhal in clean water and simmer in fresh water until tender. Drain and set on one side.

Fry the onions and garlic in the oil until they begin to colour then stir in the curry powder and ginger. Add the lime juice and the cassia or cinnamon.

Tip the cooked dhal into the pan and stir gently to coat them with the spicy mixture. Pour over 4 tablespoons of water and cover the pan. Cook very gently for 10 minutes, season with salt and fork in the coriander leaves.

Turn out onto a serving dish, remove the cassia or cinnamon and decorate with the hard-boiled eggs and a few coriander leaves.
VARIATION: Add an extra ½ litre (1 pt) water to make a thin dhal to serve with a dry main dish.

Green Dhal Tarka

For this recipe I have substituted whole green mung beans in place of the hulled split 'moong' dhal which is traditionally used in this type of dish. This is simply because the whole mung beans are more easily obtainable here though they do also add colour to the dish. 'Tarka' refers to the final addition of fried spices which gives the dhal its 'kick'.

225 g (8 oz) whole green mung beans, soaked for 1 hour in cold water
2 onions, chopped
3 cloves garlic, crushed
25 g (1 oz) ghee or butter
2 tablespoons oil
1 tablespoon grated fresh ginger
½-1 teaspoon cayenne pepper
225 g (8 oz) fresh or frozen spinach
¼ teaspoon salt
1 dessertspoon chopped mint
2 teaspoons black mustard seeds
½ teaspoon whole cumin seeds
1 teaspoon garam masala

Drain the beans and put into a pan with 750 ml (1¼ pts) of fresh cold water. Simmer gently for 30-40 minutes or until the beans are soft. Drain off any excess water and cover to keep warm.

Fry the onions and garlic in half the ghee or butter and oil, until they are coloured but still soft. Add the ginger and cayenne pepper and cook for another minute.

Chappaties and Mixed Dhal with Sesame Seeds.

If using fresh spinach, wash and remove any tough stalks. Stir the fresh or frozen spinach into the onion mixture and pour in 150 ml (¼ pt) of water and the salt. Cover the pan and simmer until the spinach is cooked, then stir in the mint and remove from the heat.

When the mixture has cooled slightly pour the entire contents of the pan into a liquidizer or food processor and blend to a thin purée. Stir this into the cooked beans and heat gently. The consistency can be varied, but traditionally it should be like a thick soup.

In a separate pan heat the remaining ghee or butter and oil and when hot add the mustard and cumin seeds. Put the lid on and cook until they 'pop'. Shake the pan over the heat and add the garam masala. Cook for a further minute, check that the green dhal mixture has warmed through then pour the oil and spices over the top and serve immediately.

The spinach and dhal can be prepared beforehand, then the tarka cooked at the last minute.

Dhals of this consistency are usually eaten with rice.

Mixed Dhal with Sesame Seeds

You can alter the pulses used in this recipe to suit whatever happens to be in your store cupboard. Pulses such as red kidney beans, chickpeas, pinto beans and butter beans which need a long cooking time should be pre-cooked and then used in place of the soaked split peas.

walnut-sized piece of tamarind or 1 teaspoon tamarind paste
2-3 green chillies, sliced
4 cloves of garlic, crushed
2 onions, finely sliced
1 tablespoon oil
50 g (2 oz) ghee or butter
2 tablespoons coriander
1 teaspoon turmeric
100 g (4 oz) yellow split peas, soaked overnight
75 g (3 oz) red lentils
2 cm (¾ in) stick of cinnamon
1 tablespoon tomato purée
3 tomatoes, quartered
2 teaspoons garam masala
salt and pepper
40 g (1½ oz) sesame seeds
2.5 cm (1 in) tender, young ginger

Pour 300 ml (½ pt) of boiling water over the tamarind and leave to soak for 10 minutes, then pour the liquid through a sieve, pushing through any pulp and discarding any hard bits.

Fry the chillies with the garlic and half of the onion in the oil and ghee or butter. Stir in the ground coriander and turmeric and cook for 1 minute. Drain the split peas and add them to the pan with the lentils, stirring well to coat them with the spices.

Pour over the tamarind water and also add the cinnamon, tomato purée, tomatoes and a further 600 ml (1 pt) of water. If using tamarind paste add it at this point.

Cover the pan and allow to simmer very gently for about ¾-1 hour or until the split peas are cooked but not mushy. The cinnamon can be removed after ½ hour for a more subtle flavour.

Sprinkle in the garam masala and salt and pepper and stir the mixture still over a gentle heat to drive off the excess moisture. Mix in the sesame seeds.

Peel the ginger and cut into thin strips. (If the ginger is tough and fibrous it is better to grate it.) In another pan fry the ginger strips and remaining onion in a little oil until brown and crisp. Keep warm.

Turn the mixed dhal out onto a serving platter and garnish with the fried onion and ginger.

Split Pea Patties

Although this recipe uses split peas, canned chickpeas or kidney beans could be used if you are short of time. These can form the main part of a vegetarian meal.

275 g (10 oz) split peas, soaked for 2 hours, or 397 g (14 oz) can of
*   cooked chickpeas or kidney beans*
oil for shallow frying
2 teaspoons whole cumin seeds
½ teaspoon whole fennel seeds
1 teaspoon turmeric
1 onion, chopped
2 cloves garlic, crushed
2 fresh green chillies, deseeded and sliced
1 dessertspoon tomato purée
1 dessertspoon chopped coriander leaves
50 g (2 oz) wholewheat flour

Drain the split peas and put into a pan with fresh water. Simmer until cooked (about 45 minutes), then drain and set on one side. If using canned pulses, simply drain them.

Heat a little oil in a pan and add the cumin and fennel seeds, cover the pan and cook until they darken in colour (about ½ minute). Stir in the turmeric, onion, garlic and chillies and fry for 5 minutes. Add the cooked pulses with the tomato purée and chopped coriander leaves.

Allow the mixture to cool and form into round patties about 10 cm (4 in) across. If the mixture is too crumbly to work with, blend quickly in a liquidizer. Dip each one into flour then fry until golden in 3-4 teaspoons of oil.

Dry Spiced Chickpeas

This is quick to make as well as being very tasty. Serve as an accompaniment or as a snack with puris.

6 cm (1½ in) piece of young tender ginger
25 g (1 oz) ghee or butter
1 tablespoon oil
1 onion, thinly sliced
397 g (14 oz) can of cooked chickpeas
½ teaspoon salt
1-2 teaspoons paprika
1 tablespoon desiccated coconut
1 teaspoon garam masala
½ lemon, squeezed

Peel the ginger and cut into thin matchsticks. (If the ginger is older and rather fibrous it is better to grate it.)

Heat the ghee or butter and oil in a heavy-bottomed pan and fry the onion and ginger until brown and crispy. Remove from the pan with a slotted spoon, leaving the remaining oil behind, and set aside.

Drain the chickpeas and dry on kitchen paper. Toss them into the pan and shake them around. Sprinkle in the salt and paprika and shake the pan over the heat for 3 minutes. Add the coconut and garam masala. The mixture will be very dry at this point and care must be taken that nothing burns. After another couple of minutes turn the heat up and pour in the lemon juice. It will sizzle and produce a cloud of steam but do not worry, as it helps the flavours to impregnate the pulses. Stir well and cook until the mixture is dry again.

Scatter the fried onion and ginger over the top and allow to cool for 5 minutes before serving.

Split Pea Patties (top left); Chickpeas with Toasted Coconut (top right); Dry Spiced Chickpeas (bottom).

Chickpeas with Toasted Coconut

Try using dried coconut shreds (available in many supermarkets and health shops) in this recipe instead of desiccated coconut. The dry nutty flavour of this dish tastes good with some of the chicken recipes, particularly the dupiaza and the Kashmiri chicken.

50 g (2 oz) shredded coconut or desiccated coconut
50 g (2 oz) ghee or butter
1 onion, finely chopped
3 cloves garlic, crushed
1 tablespoon ground coriander
400 g (14 oz) cooked chickpeas, either tinned or soaked and boiled
*   until tender*
2 dried red chillies, chopped
juice of 1 lime or lemon
1 teaspoon garam masala
salt to taste
2 tablespoons chopped fresh coriander

Heat the grill and place the coconut underneath on a baking sheet. Shake the tray around until all the coconut has turned light brown. Set on one side.

Heat the ghee or butter in a pan and fry the onion, garlic and the ground coriander. When the onion is soft stir in the chickpeas and chillies along with the lemon or lime juice. Season with salt and cover the pan. Simmer gently for 10 minutes.

Add the garam masala, salt and half of the toasted coconut and cook, uncovered, until quite dry.

Garnish with the chopped coriander and the rest of the coconut.

Kitcherie

The rice and smoked haddock kedgeree which we all know is a distant relative of the Indian kitcherie. Traditionally made with rice and lentils it is quite a mild dish. In the days of the British Raj in India this may well have been one of the first things that the colonials dared to try and then went on to adapt and adopt it as their own.

175 g (6 oz) long grain rice
175 g (6 oz) split peas
1 onion, finely sliced
75 g (3 oz) ghee or butter
1 bay leaf
1 tablespoon tender fresh ginger, cut into thin sticks
½ teaspoon garam masala (optional)
750 ml (1¼ pts) vegetable or chicken stock
½ teaspoon salt

Wash the rice and split peas and allow them to soak in cold water for ½ hour.

Fry the onion in the ghee or butter until pale golden coloured. Stir in the bay leaf, ginger and drained split peas and cook for 5 minutes, stirring all the time. Add the rice and fry for 1 minute. If using garam masala stir it in at this point. Pour the stock over and allow to come up to the boil. Lower the heat, cover the pan and simmer as gently as possible until the rice is well done and the split peas are just soft. Drive off any excess moisture by cooking briefly with the lid off. Season with salt and turn out onto a serving dish.

Plain Rice

The method of gentle simmering and steaming is the one most
favoured in India and produces light separate grains of rice.
The quantity of water required will vary according to which
type of rice you use, but with a little experience you will soon
know exactly how much is needed. Choose a good patna rice. If
you prefer brown, unpolished rice for its higher nutritional
content, choose long, slim grains.

200 g (7 oz) long grain white or brown rice
475 ml (16 fl oz) water for white rice or 725 ml (24 fl oz) for brown rice
pinch of salt

Wash the rice and allow to soak in clean water for 1-2 hours if possible.

Rinse and put into a lidded pan with cold water and salt. Bring to
the boil then stir a couple of times and cover tightly with the lid.
Reduce the heat to its lowest setting and leave the pan for 12-15
minutes for white rice or 30-40 minutes for brown. It is important not
to take the lid off during the cooking time as valuable steam escapes.
At the end of the cooking time the rice should be just cooked and all
the liquid absorbed. Turn onto a serving platter and serve at once.

To reheat rice, place in an ovenproof dish and cover tightly with
foil. Heat for 15 minutes at Gas Mark 6, 380°F, 200°C.

Pullau Rice

This rice dish can be served with meat or vegetable dishes and
also forms the base of some more complicated recipes like
biriani, where cooked meat is added to it. It comes from the
north of India and you will recognize the use of strong, whole
spices. The addition of fruit and nuts is a Persian influence
dating from the days of the Mogul Empire. The rice is very rich
and some recipes call for equal quantities of rice and ghee or
butter. For everyday cooking I have reduced the fat content
somewhat, but do urge you to use ghee for this recipe if
possible.

350 g (12 oz) basmati rice
2 small onions
100 g (4 oz) ghee or butter
2 cloves garlic, crushed
5 whole green cardamom pods
4 whole cloves
2-3 cm (1 in) stick of cinnamon
2 teaspoons whole all-spice
75 g (3 oz) sultanas or raisins
75 g (3 oz) whole almonds, skinned
½ teaspoon salt (optional)

Lemon Rice

**This is a simple way to make rice more interesting without
going to a great deal of trouble. It can be served with most
meals, but is especially good served with Tandoori Chicken
or Chicken Tikka.**

350 g (12 oz) long grain rice
½ teaspoon salt
½ teaspoon turmeric
50 g (2 oz) butter
juice of 1 large lemon
150 ml (¼ pt) plain yoghurt
1 dessertspoon fresh mint, chopped

Wash the rice and allow to stand in cold water for ½-1 hour, then
drain.

Bring a large pan of salted water to the boil. Sprinkle in the
turmeric and the drained rice. Cook for about 10-12 minutes until the
rice is just cooked. The time will depend upon the type of rice used.

While the rice is cooking melt the butter and add the lemon juice,
yoghurt and mint.

Drain the rice and add to the lemony mixture. Stir until it is all
mixed together then turn out onto a serving platter.

Exotic Spiced Rice

**This is a type of special pullau rice which would only be served
at feasts or weddings. Here is an opportunity to try some of the
tropical fruits now available in our greengrocers and
supermarkets. Fresh fruit is essential, as the canned fruits
have often lost their texture and flavour. Serve this rice with a
selection of meat and vegetable dishes at a dinner party and
your guests will feel they have eaten like kings.**

350 g (12 oz) basmati rice
4 apricots
1 mango
1 small papaya
½ small pineapple
1 large onion, sliced
1 tablespoon fresh ginger, grated
75 g (3 oz) ghee or butter
2 teaspoons ground cumin
¼ teaspoon freshly ground black pepper
2-3 cm (1 in) stick of cinnamon
10 green cardamom pods
few strands saffron, soaked in 5 tablespoons of warm milk
100 g (4 oz) mixed cashew, pistachio and almonds

Wash the rice and allow to stand in cold water for ½ hour. Stone and
slice the apricots. Peel the mango and cut into chunks, discarding the
stone. Peel the papaya, cut in half, remove the seeds and slice the
flesh. Peel the pineapple, removing the 'eyes' with the skin and cut the
fruit into chunks.

Fry the onion and ginger in the ghee or butter until soft. Add the
cumin, pepper, cinnamon and cardamoms and fry for 2 minutes. Stir
in the rice with a pinch of salt. Cook for 5 minutes then pour over
boiling water to cover the rice by about 5 cm (2 in). Stir well then
cover and cook for 6 minutes. Pour the saffron infused milk over the
rice to make pretty orange zigzags. Do not stir it in, as the purpose is to
colour and flavour only some of the rice. Replace the lid and continue
to cook until the rice is tender and all of the water has been absorbed.

Stir in some of the fruit and nuts and use the rest as garnish.

Exotic Spiced Rice.

Wash the rice and stand in cold water for between 30 minutes and 2
hours. (This reduces the starch content of the rice.)

Slice one onion into thin rings. Top and tail the other onion and
cut it into four lengthwise. Separate out the onion layers to give petal
shapes.

Fry the onion rings in a little ghee or butter until crisp and
brown. Remove from the pan with a slotted spoon and keep warm.
Add the rest of the ghee or butter and fry the onion 'petals' and garlic
until soft but still pale in colour.

Drain the rice and stir into the pan with the garlic and all the
spices. Cook gently until the rice becomes translucent. This will take
about 5 minutes and the ghee or butter should not be more than pale
golden in colour. Pour in boiling water to cover the rice by about 5 cm
(2 in). Stir in the sultanas and almonds and cover tightly. Add the salt
if using.

Cook very slowly until all the liquid has been absorbed yet the
grains of rice are still separate and certainly not mushy. A very quick
peep at the rice is allowed after 10 minutes, just to reassure yourself,
but when you have made the dish a few times you will be able to gauge
the cooking time required. A lot depends upon how low you can set
your hob.

Serve garnished with the fried onion rings.

Accompaniments

No Indian meal would be complete without at least one, preferably several, chutneys, sambals or pickles served with it. Variations are endless, with individual cooks priding themselves on their own specialities.

Poppadums are popular throughout India. They are sometimes eaten as a starter with fresh coriander or mint chutney or placed in a stack on the table to munch with the main event.

Chutneys fall into two categories, uncooked and preserved. Mango chutney is the most famous preserved chutney. Uncooked chutneys are more like raitas; they often use yoghurt as their base and ground spices, herbs or other fresh ingredients are mixed in. Unlike the raitas, which soothe the palate, fresh chutneys are a tasty part of the meal.

Sambals (egg, potato, prawn and so on) can be likened to side salads, though naturally they tend to include some garam masala, cayenne pepper or fresh chillies. Formal recipes for these are rare in India as cooks generally use whatever is in the kitchen and vary the seasoning to suit the main dishes.

To a Western palate all Indian pickles are hot, but to taste buds brought up on a highly spiced diet only the awesome pickled chillies are really considered fiery. This section includes recipes for prawn pickle and lemon and lime pickle, either of which can be served with any Indian meal to provide an extra zip. Eaten in modest quantities pickles should stimulate the appetite and promote a feeling of well-being.

Unlike classical French cuisine there are no firm rules regarding the garnishing of Indian dishes. For special occasions, weddings and banquets for example, sweets may have a thin covering of gold or silver leaf (vaark) which is edible and looks very grand. Individual squares of gold and silver leaf are available from specialist Indian shops and also from cake decorating suppliers. For savoury dishes use raw or fried onion rings, sliced tomato or cucumber, chopped parsley or leaf coriander as decoration. Wedges of lemon or lime complement fish recipes particularly well and toasted almonds and lightly fried sultanas can also be used to good effect.

Fresh Coconut Chutney

The abundance of coconuts in southern India means that they find their way into all areas of cookery. This recipe is popular and very simple to make. Many variations exist, some of which are listed for you to try. Coconut Chutney can be served with any Indian meal and is ideal to accompany snacks.

½ fresh coconut, grated or 50 g (2 oz) desiccated coconut, preferably unsweetened
1-2 fresh green chillies, deseeded and chopped
2 cloves garlic, crushed
1 teaspoon grated fresh ginger
3 tablespoons lemon or lime juice
salt and pepper to taste

Place all the ingredients in a liquidizer or food processor and blend until smooth. This can also be done using a pestle and mortar if you do not have a food processor.

VARIATIONS
Omit the chillies for a milder flavour.
Substitute a little tamarind liquid for the lime or lemon juice.
Add one or more of the following:
Chopped fresh coriander or mint leaves
Garam masala
Dry roasted and ground cumin seeds
Stem ginger
Pinch of turmeric for colour
Fried mustard seeds

Spicy Mango Chutney

As the cost of mangos is rather prohibitive, I have supplemented half of their weight for cooking apples. This chutney should be allowed to mellow and mature for a month or two. It is very good and you will not be tempted with 'shop' chutney once you've tried this one.

900 g (2 lb) green mangos
600 ml (1 pt) water
50 g (2 oz) salt
50 g (2 oz) tender fresh ginger
900 g (2 lb) cooking apples
450 g (1 lb) light brown sugar
600 ml (1 pt) white malt vinegar
1-2 teaspoons chilli powder
2 cinnamon sticks
3 teaspoons whole mustard seeds
5 cloves garlic, peeled and sliced

Peel the mangos and cut the flesh into chunks. Discard the skin and put the chunks of mango and their stones into a bowl with the water. Sprinkle all the salt over and leave for 12 to 24 hours.

Peel the ginger and if it is very tender cut it into thin slices. If it feels tough and fibrous it is better to grate it. Peel the cooking apples, core them and cut into chunks.

Put the sugar and vinegar in a large, heavy pan and heat slowly until the sugar has dissolved. Bring to the boil and let it bubble gently for 10 minutes.

Drain the mango and add to the pan with all the other ingredients. Bring back to the boil, then lower the heat and simmer as gently as possible for 1 to 1½ hours or until thick. Stir the pan every 5 minutes or more if the mixture begins to stick to the bottom of the pan. Cool for 5 minutes.

Have some clean, warmed jam jars ready and ladle the chutney into them while it is still warm. Cover the top of the chutney with waxed discs, seal and label.

Chicken Tikka Kebabs (page 18), with Spicy Mango Chutney and Lemon Rice (page 67).

Clockwise from top left: *Capsicum Sambal, Prawn Sambal; Potato Sambal; Aubergine Sambal; Egg Sambal; Tomato and Onion Sambal; Coconut Sambal.*

Sambals

These are simple side dishes which often accompany a main meal. They should have a clean refreshing taste, like a side salad and the variations are literally endless. Bear in mind colours, taste and textures when choosing Sambals and feel free to invent your own specialities.

Tomato and Onion Sambal

2 tomatoes, skinned and sliced
1 dessertspoon chopped spring onions
1 tablespoon lemon juice
1 dessertspoon desiccated coconut
cayenne pepper, salt and pepper to taste

Mix all the ingredients together. Chill before serving.

Egg Sambal

2-3 hard-boiled eggs, peeled and quartered
1 tablespoon finely chopped onion
½ teaspoon paprika or chopped green chillies
2 teaspoons poppy seeds
2 tablespoons plain yoghurt
salt and plenty of freshly ground black pepper

Mix the seasonings with the yoghurt and spoon over the eggs. Leave for ½ hour before serving.

Prawn Sambal

100 g (4 oz) prawns
25 g (1 oz) ghee or butter
15 g (½ oz) creamed coconut
1 teaspoon tomato purée
½ teaspoon garam masala
1 lemon
salt and pepper
1 tablespoon chopped onion
1 dessertspoon chopped coriander leaves

Fry the prawns lightly in the ghee or butter and stir in the creamed coconut and tomato purée. Sprinkle in the garam masala and cook for a further minute. Allow to cool, and then thin the sambal a little with the juice of half a lemon. Season with the salt and pepper and mix in the raw onion and coriander. Serve garnished with dainty lemon wedges.

Potato Sambal

100 g (4 oz) cooked potatoes, diced
1 teaspoon chopped fresh green chillies
1 dessertspoon snipped chives
1-2 tablespoons salad oil
2 tablespoons chopped cashew nuts
2 tablespoons raisins
salt and pepper to taste
1 teaspoon garam masala

Combine all the ingredients together, sprinkling the garam masala on top at the last minute.

Capsicum Sambal

1 small green pepper
1 small red or yellow pepper
2 teaspoons cumin seeds, dry roasted, then ground
1 teaspoon crushed garlic
¼-½ teaspoon paprika
salt and pepper to taste
2 tablespoons salad oil

Wash and dry the capsicums. Cook them whole under a hot grill until the skin is charred all over. Let them cool slightly then peel or rub off the skin. Remove the stalk and seeds and slice the flesh into thin strips. Stir in the cumin, garlic, paprika and salt and pepper. Spoon into a side dish and sprinkle with oil. Chill for an hour before serving.

Aubergine Sambal

1 medium aubergine
15 g (½ oz) creamed coconut
3 tablespoons plain yoghurt
1 teaspoon crushed garlic
1 dessertspoon chopped parsley
salt and pepper to taste

If you happen to be using the oven pop the aubergine in whole and cook until it is cooked through and feels soft. Turn the grill to maximum and char the skin of the cooked aubergine. Alternatively, grill the raw aubergine using a moderate heat until it is cooked through and the skin is blackened and crisp. Rub off the skin using an old, clean tea towel. Chop the flesh finely. Melt the creamed coconut and stir in the yoghurt. Add the aubergine along with the rest of the ingredients. Chill before serving.

Coconut Sambal

150 ml (¼ pt) plain yoghurt
½ fresh coconut, grated
1 teaspoon chopped chillies
1 teaspoon crushed garlic
½ teaspoon turmeric
1 teaspoon dry roasted ground cumin seeds
pinch of sugar

Blend all the ingredients to a paste in a liquidizer. Season with salt and pepper to taste.

Prawn Pickle

Use this to accompany any main meal but it is particularly good with spiced fish dishes. After opening, store in the refrigerator.

300 ml (½ pt) sesame seed, mustard or vegetable oil
2 onions, finely sliced
3 cloves garlic, finely sliced
4 cm (1½ in) piece of fresh ginger, finely sliced
2-4 dried red chillies, finely sliced
2 teaspoons turmeric
2 teaspoons ground cumin
1 teaspoon mustard seeds
2 teaspoons garam masala
3 tablespoons vinegar
3 tablespoons lemon juice
350 g (12 oz) prawns, roughly chopped
75 g (3 oz) desiccated coconut
1 tablespoon chopped coriander leaves
1 teaspoon salt

Heat ¼ of the oil in a saucepan and add the onions, garlic, ginger, chillies, turmeric, cumin, mustard seeds and garam masala. Cover the pan and cook gently for 6 minutes or until the onion is soft but not coloured. Stir in the vinegar, lemon juice and the rest of the oil. Gradually increase the heat until the mixture begins to simmer. Cook and stir for 3 minutes then remove from the heat.

Add the prawns, coconut, coriander and salt to the pan. Cool completely. Spoon the pickle into clean jam jars and seal. Keep for a week before using to let the flavour develop. Eat within 5-6 weeks.

Poppadums

Known variously as papads, pappadums and papars, these crisp wafer-like biscuits are ideal cocktail fare or can be served with a meal. They are fairly laborious to make and even in India they are usually bought ready made. Varieties of Poppadums range from plain, unspiced ones through to very hot types red with chillies.

To cook ready made poppadums, place under a hot grill for about 30 seconds on each side or until they turn crisp and begin to brown.

Alternatively they can be fried in a pan containing about 2-3 cm (1 in) of hot oil. Have a fish slice handy and lay one poppadum in the pan. Hold it down with the slice to completely submerge it for a couple of seconds then quickly turn it over. The poppadum will expand and be cooked in 5-10 seconds. Remove from the pan and lay on a piece of kitchen paper to absorb excess oil. Fried poppadums tend to be lighter and crisper than grilled ones, but they are rather more greasy.

Cooked poppadums can be kept warm in the oven until required.

Lemon and Lime Pickle

Choose small, thin-skinned lemons for this or use all limes, the skins of which soften more quickly. Mustard oil is best for pickles, but can be difficult to find. Sesame seed oil is good, but is expensive. Alternatively, use vegetable oil.

3 lemons
3 limes
40 g (1½ oz) rock salt
3 cloves garlic
2 fresh green chillies
2-3 cm (1 in) piece peeled fresh ginger
1 teaspoon freshly ground black pepper
1 teaspoon ground fenugreek seeds
120 ml (4 fl oz) mustard, sesame or vegetable oil
1 tablespoon mustard seeds

Wash and dry the fruit and cut into slim wedges or chunks. Place in a bowl, sprinkle with the salt and leave for 12 hours.

Chop the garlic into small pieces, but do not crush. Slice the chillies and the peeled ginger finely. Mix these in with the fruit and add the pepper and fenugreek.

Heat 1 tablespoon of the oil and fry the mustard seeds until they pop, keeping the lid on until they have stopped sputtering. Take care not to burn the oil. Add the rest of the oil and heat until it just begins to smoke. Remove from the heat immediately.

Pack the lemons and limes into a sterilized, dry jar along with all the flavourings and when cool, pour the oil and mustard seeds in until the jar is full.

During the summer leave the pickle in sunlight, covered with a piece of muslin or cheesecloth during the daytime for 1 week. At night stir the pickle and put the lid on.

If you make this in winter, or during a dull summer, keep the pickle in a warm dry place, such as an airing cupboard, and cover and stir as for summer. Do bear in mind the aroma which will waft its way into your linen or ironing.

The pickle is ready to eat when the skins of the fruit are soft. It will take between 2-4 weeks depending on the amount of sunshine it receives. Once it is ready store the pickle in the refrigerator. Serve small amounts of the fruit, leaving the oil in the jar.

As with most pickles, this one improves with age.

Raitas

These yoghurt-based relishes can be served with any Indian meal. At its simplest a raita can consist of lightly beaten yoghurt seasoned with salt and freshly ground black pepper. Here are some variations on the theme but there are no hard and fast rules so do invent your own speciality. Chillies, paprika or cayenne pepper can be added, but as Raitas are often served to counteract the fieriness of a dish it is as well to steer towards clean, refreshing flavours.

Celery and Walnut Raita
150 ml (¼ pt) plain yoghurt
2 sticks celery, very thinly sliced
25 g (1 oz) walnuts, chopped
a few chopped coriander leaves
salt and freshly ground black pepper

Beat the yoghurt lightly with a fork then stir in the celery, nuts and coriander leaves. Season with salt and pepper and chill before serving.

Fresh Tomato Chutney

This uncooked chutney can be served like a side salad with a wide variety of Indian dishes. Try it with dry spicy main dishes such as Barbecued Chicken, Spit Roasted Game Birds or Cashew Stuffed Trout. Avoid using pale tomatoes as their flesh is often quite tasteless   1 choose instead firm bright red ones.

4 tomatoes, skinned
½ cucumber
1 tablespoon chopped coriander leaves
1 tablespoon finely chopped onion
½ teaspoon paprika or finely chopped green chillies
2 tablespoons salad oil
lemon or lime juice to taste
salt and pepper

Slice or chop the tomatoes and cucumber, removing the seeds if desired. Mix together with all the other ingredients and chill for an hour before serving.

Variations
For a more exotic chutney try adding one or all of the following:
Sultanas lightly fried in butter
Toasted flaked almonds
1 teaspoon dry roasted ground cumin seeds

Green Chutney

This fresh chutney, usually called Podina, is one of the few found in Indian restaurants abroad. Sometimes it is served with a couple of poppadums as an appetizer or it can be used as an adjunct to almost any Indian main course.

2 handfuls fresh mint leaves
2 tablespoons chopped coriander leaves
1 teaspoon chopped green chilli (optional)
1 teaspoon sugar
½ teaspoon salt
4 tablespoons lime juice
pinch of garam masala
freshly ground black pepper to taste

Blend all the ingredients together in a liquidizer, or grind using a pestle and mortar to give a bright green paste.

Bombay Duck

The outstanding feature of Bombay ducks is that they are, in fact, fish. Properly known as bummelo or bombloe fish, they are to be found in the coastal waters around Bombay. They earn their nickname from swimming just under or on the surface of the sea. In India they can be bought fresh but here they are only available dried and salted and are most often grilled or fried. They can then be crumbled over other dishes or served as an appetizer. Bombay ducks can be bought from Indian shops or good delicatessens.

Banana Raita
2 medium bananas, sliced
1-2 tablespoons lemon juice
150 ml (¼ pt) plain yoghurt
25 g (1 oz) sultanas
½ teaspoon garam masala
salt and pepper

Sprinkle the bananas with the lemon juice. Lightly beat the yoghurt and mix with all the other ingredients. Chill before serving.

Cucumber and Capsicum Raita
150 ml (¼ pt) plain yoghurt
1 green pepper, de-seeded and thinly sliced
¾ large cucumber, washed and diced
1 tablespoon chopped coriander leaves
2 teaspoons sesame seeds
salt and pepper

Lightly beat the yoghurt, stir in the prepared vegetables, coriander leaves and sesame seeds and season with salt and pepper. Chill for about 1 hour before serving.

Sweets and Desserts

In India sweetmeats are sold in specialist shops or by street traders. The shops are very tempting, with shelves piled high with neat, colourful merchandise – trays of round ladoos of all flavours, stacks of green pistachio or creamy almond burfi delicately coated with thin gold and silver leaf and big glass jars full of milk sweets floating in rose-scented syrup. These traditional milk and ground nut delicacies are popular with young and old alike. They are given as gifts to guests or are served at banquets and weddings or simply eaten as snacks. Although these sweets are very rich they are all made with natural ingredients and are eaten in small quantities.

Sometimes a dessert will be served after a main meal but peeled and sliced fresh fruit is more usual. In parts of India a sweet or bowl of kheer is produced at the beginning of the meal as an appetizer. Unless you have tried it, you might think that kheer is just another rice pudding but in fact it is quite delicious.

Many of the sweets have a milk base. In some cases the milk is cooked in a thick pan for an hour or more until all that remains is a stiff white paste known as khoiya. In others the milk is soured with lemon juice then strained through muslin to make paneer. An alternative method for making khoiya is to mix full cream powdered milk with a little hot water.

Sweet Vermicelli

This is a fairly simple dessert which can be eaten hot or cold. The Italian-style vermicelli available in supermarkets is suitable for this dish.

100 g (4 oz) ghee or butter
100 g (4 oz) vermicelli
1 l (2 pts) milk
few strands of saffron
140 g (5 oz) sugar
75 g (3 oz) raisins
75 g (3 oz) flaked almonds
1 teaspoon ground cardamom
1 teaspoon rose water or few drops of kevda or kewra water

Heat the ghee or butter in a large saucepan. Break the vermicelli nests in half and add them to the pan. Stir gently until the vermicelli begins to colour, then lift out and place in a second pan. Pour the hot milk over the vermicelli and bring to the boil. Reduce the heat, sprinkle in the saffron and allow to simmer gently for 10 minutes. Add the sugar and simmer for another 10 minutes.

Meanwhile reheat the ghee in the pan and fry the raisins and nuts with the cardamom. Reserve some of the fried fruit and nuts for garnishing and stir the rest into the cooked vermicelli along with any ghee left in the pan.

Either serve hot, sprinkled with a little of the flavoured water of your choice and the reserved fruit and nuts, or pour into a serving dish and allow to cool. When the mixture is cold it will thicken. A couple of spoonfuls of cream stirred in just before serving make this really delicious. Garnish as before with the flavouring, fruit and nuts.

Bombay Pudding

This type of dish may be made in advance then quickly fried in butter just before serving. It makes a lovely afternoon snack and is usually eaten with a little flavoured syrup. If you are short of time substitute warm golden syrup mixed with lemon juice and omit the syrup part of the recipe.

1 large can evaporated milk
300 ml (½ pt) milk
100 g (4 oz) ground rice
75 g (3 oz) butter
2 tablespoons thick honey

Syrup
75 g (3 oz) granulated sugar
150 ml (¼ pt) water
pared rind of half a lemon or 4 cardamom pods

Put the evaporated milk, milk and ground rice in a pan. Bring to the boil and simmer until very thick and leaving the sides of the pan. Stir in half the butter and the honey. Tip out onto a shallow dish and smooth over. Cover with cling film and leave until cold and set.

Turn out onto a floured cloth and cut into 6-8 wedges. Heat the remaining butter and gently fry the slices of pudding until golden brown on both sides and warmed through. Serve with a little syrup.

To make the syrup put the sugar, water and lemon rind or cardamom pods into a pan. Bring to the boil slowly, then boil for 6-8 minutes. Strain and serve.

Banana and Pineapple Fritters

All types of fritters are eaten in India. These are simple to make and are best eaten straight away. Try them on their own, or serve them with cream, honey or syrup for a delicious dessert.

3 ripe bananas
75 g (3 oz) self-raising flour
40 g (1½ oz) soft brown sugar
pinch of all-spice
milk
50 g (2 oz) chopped pineapple
oil for deep frying

Mash 2 of the bananas and mix with the flour, sugar and all-spice. Stir in enough milk to form a thick batter.

Chop the other banana and drain the pineapple. Stir them into the batter. Heat the oil and deep fry spoonfuls of the mixture until golden brown. Drain then dust with caster sugar.

Sweet Vermicelli.

Almond and Pistachio Burfi

Burfis are rich sweetmeats which are eaten on special occasions or boxed and given as presents. Although sometimes homemade, they are usually bought from specialist shops which have dazzling displays of mouth-watering sweets. Traditionally burfis are coated with vaark – thin gold or silver leaf. A silver dishful of these sweets handed round after dinner will be much appreciated.

425 g (15 oz) granulated sugar
360 ml (12 fl oz) water
275 g (10 oz) full cream powdered milk
175 g (6 oz) ground almonds
1 teaspoon ground cardamom
175 g (6 oz) ground unsalted pistachios
few drops green food colouring (optional)
25 g (1 oz) mixed almonds and pistachios

Put the sugar and water into a pan and heat gently until the sugar has dissolved. Boil rapidly until the syrup reaches 240°C or until it has thickened slightly.

Divide the milk powder evenly between two bowls. Stir the ground almonds and half of the cardamom into one bowl and the ground pistachios and remaining cardamom into the other. Gradually pour half of the syrup into the almond mixture and work in to form a stiff paste.

Colour the remaining syrup light green and work it into the pistachio mixture to form a stiff paste.

Line a square tin with greaseproof paper and brush with oil. Press the almond mixture into the tin and spread the green burfi evenly on top. Press lightly with the back of a spoon.

Cut the almonds and pistachios into fine slivers and use these to stud the surface. When cold and set cut into small square or diamond shapes and ease out of the tin.

Kheer

Kheers are highly regarded in India and have many variations. For a plain Kheer omit the sultanas and creamed coconut. Whole cracked cardamom pods can be used in place of the ground cardamom powder, but remember to remove them before serving. Traditionally this dish is decorated with vaark, thin gold or silver leaf which is edible, and served chilled.

1 l (2 pts) full cream milk
1 heaped tablespoon basmati rice
1 teaspoon ground cardamom powder
25 g (1 oz) creamed coconut
25 g (1 oz) sultanas
40 g (1½ oz) sugar
50 g (2 oz) chopped almonds
50 g (2 oz) chopped pistachio nuts
1 teaspoon rose water

Pour the milk into a large pan and add the rice. Bring to the boil then simmer gently for ½ hour. Add the ground cardamom and creamed coconut and simmer for a further ½ hour. Add the sultanas, sugar and most of the nuts. Simmer for 10 minutes or until thick.

Pour into a serving dish and allow to cool completely. Sprinkle the top with rose water and decorate with the chopped almonds and pistachios.

Indian Seed Cake

Seed cake (also known as beveca) is Anglo-Indian in origin and works very well. Served sliced it makes an unusual teatime treat.

100 g (4 oz) butter
225 g (8 oz) sugar
4 eggs, beaten
25 g (1 oz) ground almonds
100 g (4 oz) plain flour
50 g (2 oz) ground rice
50 g (2 oz) fine semolina
50 g (2 oz) desiccated coconut
1 teaspoon ground cardamom seeds
milk
15 g (½ oz) caraway seeds
15 g (½ oz) sesame seeds

Soften the butter in a bowl and work in the sugar. Beat until light and fluffy. Gradually beat the eggs into the mixture.

Fold in the ground almonds, flour, ground rice, semolina, desiccated coconut and cardamom powder. Stir in a little milk to make a soft dropping consistency. Spoon into the buttered tin and sprinkle the caraway and sesame seeds over the top. Bake at Gas Mark 4, 180°C, 360°F until light brown and set. Cool in the tin then cut into dainty fingers.

Indian Seed Cake (top); Almond and Pistachio Burfi (bottom).

Shrikand

This is a delightfully fragrant yoghurt dish, variations of which are enjoyed all over India. Sometimes small bowls of Shrikand are served at the beginning of a meal with hot puris. You may prefer to serve it as a dessert.

1 l (2 pts) thick plain yoghurt
1 tablespoon milk
few strands of saffron
25 g (1 oz) almonds
25 g (1 oz) pistachios or cashew nuts
2 teaspoons ground cardamom seeds
50 g (2 oz) caster sugar
1 tablespoon thick honey
½ teaspoon rose water

Put the yoghurt into a jelly bag or a clean piece of muslin tied at the corners and hang over a bowl to allow excess liquid to drain away. This will take up to 4-5 hours depending on the thickness of the yoghurt.

Heat the milk and pour over the saffron, leave it to infuse for 1 hour, then strain. Meanwhile pour boiling water over the almonds and pistachios or cashew nuts and leave them to soak for 10 minutes. Drain the nuts and slice thinly.

Turn the yoghurt out into a bowl and stir in the ground cardamom, sugar, honey and strained saffron milk. Spoon into a serving dish. Sprinkle the surface with the rose water and scatter the sliced nuts over the top. Chill very well before serving.

Quick Kulfi

Kulfi is India's national ice cream. It is usually sold as an ice lolly on a stick and is slim and conical in shape. Partly because freezers are still not commonplace in India and also because of the time involved in making kulfi, it is not normally made in the home. This recipe is definitely not the traditional method. I have replaced the lengthy process of boiling down milk, which can take up to 2 hours, with the quicker task of opening a can of evaporated milk. To the purists, I apologise, but hope you will try it anyway.

410 g (14½ fl oz) can of evaporated milk
1 level tablespoon ground rice or cornflour
75 g (3 oz) caster sugar
50 g (2 oz) full cream powdered milk
40 g (1½ oz) ground almonds
5 cardamom pods
50 g (2 oz) flaked almonds or unsalted sliced pistachios

Pour the evaporated milk into a saucepan and warm gently. Mix the ground rice or cornflour with a little water to form a paste and add to the pan. Stir until it thickens. Sprinkle in the sugar, powdered milk and ground almonds and simmer for 5 minutes. Take care that the mixture does not burn on the base of the pan.

Crack open the cardamom pods, remove the seeds and grind them to a powder. Stir this into the kulfi. Allow to cool, then cover with cling wrap and place in the freezer.

Let the kulfi freeze around the edge of the dish, then take it out and beat thoroughly. It will be quite stiff at this stage. Spoon into individual cartons or one larger bowl, scatter the nuts on top and freeze until completely set.

Allow to stand for at least 5 minutes at room temperature before serving.

Carrot Halva

This is a lovely homemade sweet with a distinctive flavour. Serve warm as a dessert or cold as a snack. If using young sweet carrots the quantity of sugar should be reduced by up to one third.

¾ l (1½ pts) whole milk
350 g (12 oz) grated carrots
pinch of nutmeg
pinch of cardamom powder
pinch of ground all-spice
100 g (4 oz) sugar
50 g (2 oz) butter
25 g (1 oz) sultanas

Put the milk into a heavy-bottomed pan and bring to the boil. Stir in the carrots and simmer very gently for ½ hour. Add the spices and continue to cook slowly, stirring every few minutes until the liquid has completely evaporated. Stir in the sugar, butter and sultanas and keep stirring over the heat for 10 minutes. By this stage the mixture should be a translucent red and all the butter absorbed.

Serve small portions warm. Alternatively, turn into an oiled tin. Press down with the back of a spoon, cool and cut into squares. Keep in an airtight tin.

Rasgullas

Rasgullas are soft cream cheese balls which have been poached in sugar syrup. They are a great favourite and are eaten either as a snack or at the end of a meal.

1¼ l (2½ pts) milk
3 tablespoons lemon juice
1 tablespoon fine semolina
a few sugar lumps
50 g (2 oz) chopped almonds
450 g (1 lb) granulated sugar
1 l (2 pts) water
6 cardamom pods or 1 teaspoon cardamom seeds
2 teaspoons rose water

Pour the milk into a saucepan and bring to the boil. Warm the lemon juice and pour into the pan. Return to the boil and stir continuously until the milk has curdled. Pour the contents of the pan through a jelly bag or a clean piece of muslin and hang up over a bowl for 12 hours to let all the liquid drain away. The soft white 'cheese' is called paneer.

When the cheese is quite dry, thoroughly mix in the semolina and knead lightly. Shape into about 10 round balls.

Break the sugar lumps into small pieces and press a piece of sugar and a few chopped nuts into the centre of each ball, carefully reshaping them afterwards. Chill for 20 minutes in the refrigerator.

Meanwhile prepare the syrup. Dissolve the sugar in the water slowly then boil steadily for 10 minutes. Pour one third of the syrup into a serving dish and set aside. Crack open the cardamom pods if using. Add the cardamom to the pan.

Slip the rasgullas into the simmering syrup and poach them gently for about an hour. As the rasgullas cook the syrup will evaporate and thicken. To prevent this happening add a little boiling water every 10 minutes.

When they are cooked remove them with a slotted spoon and lift them into the fresh syrup. Stir in the rose water and eat warm or chilled.

Mango Fool

This light dessert is ideal for rounding off a special Indian meal.

300 ml (½ pt) thick plain yoghurt
450 g (1 lb) chopped mango flesh
75 g (3 oz) sugar
½ teaspoon ground cardamom
1 tablespoon honey
150 ml (¼ pt) double cream (optional)
1 tablespoon lemon or lime juice
25 g (1 oz) toasted coconut
25 g (1 oz) toasted flaked almonds

Put the yoghurt in a piece of muslin, draw up the corners and hang above a bowl. Let the moisture drain out of the yoghurt for 2 hours. A jelly bag is an effective substitute for the muslin.

Put the mango, sugar and ground cardamom into a pan, cover and simmer for 5-6 minutes. Blend the mixture to a smooth purée in a liquidizer, press through a sieve, then cool in a bowl.

When the fruit is cold mix in the strained yoghurt and honey. Whip the cream until thick then carefully fold into the mango mixture. Add lemon or lime juice to taste and pour into a serving dish or individual glasses. Chill well. Just before serving scatter the coconut and almonds over the top.

Fresh Fruit

The climatic variations in a country as vast as India means that many types of fruit can grow there. Some are native to India others have been successfully introduced but people tend to eat locally grown produce so not all the varieties are available to all the population. Many of these are now available here, although the cost of importing them often makes them rather expensive. Fresh fruit makes a pleasant ending to a rich meal and below is a list of how to deal with some of the more unusual fruits.

Guavas

A greenish-yellow fruit about the size of a tangerine. The skin is inedible so cut the guava in half and use a teaspoon to scoop out the pale flesh and sweet seeds. A ripe guava should be slightly soft but not squashy.

Limes

These look like small bright green lemons and are a tropical citrus fruit. They can be used in place of lemons although they have a stronger flavour. Because they are smaller and have thinner skins than lemons they tend to dry out more quickly so choose plump limes with smooth skins.

Chickoos (also known as Sapodilla plum)

Tangerine-sized round fruit, chickoos have a strong treacle-like aroma and flavour. They have a rough brown skin and yellow-brown flesh. Cut them in half, discard the seeds and eat the flesh only with a teaspoon.

Mangos

These are the best-loved Indian fruit. The Alphonso variety is the most highly prized. They are oval or kidney shaped and can weigh up to 450 g (1 lb) each. The thin skin turns from green through to orange-red as they ripen. Mangos need to be peeled before eating, then sliced around the long slim stone. If the mango is ripe the stone can be eased out of the flesh but more often the flesh has to be sliced off, leaving some stuck to the stone. The best way to deal with this is to suck and nibble the stone. The yellow flesh is juicy, fibrous and very sweet. Indian children eat the unripe fruit dipped into chilli powder and salt which is definitely an acquired taste!

Papaya (also known as pawpaw)

The pear-shaped papaya has a very distinctive flavour. The smooth skin turns yellow as the fruit ripens but should still feel firm. Cut the papaya in half lengthwise and scoop out the cluster of shiny brown seeds and discard them. Peel off the skin and cut the pink coloured flesh into wedges. Serve sprinkled with lime juice and sugar.

Pummelo

This is a citrus fruit related to the grapefruit but is much larger. The skin and pith is extremely thick and the fruit is very sour.

Gulab Jamun

This sweetmeat consists of deep-fried paste balls soaked in a fragrant syrup. It is very sweet, but one or two jamuns round off a spicy meal perfectly. They can be served chilled or warm with a little accompanying syrup.

675 g (1½ lb) granulated sugar
1½ l (3 pts) water
6 cracked cardamom pods
2-3 teaspoons rose water
75 g (3 oz) ground almonds
75 g (3 oz) full cream milk powder
140 g (5 oz) fine semolina
25 g (1 oz) plain flour
1 teaspoon baking powder
50 g (2 oz) ghee or butter
2 eggs, beaten
12 blanched almonds, split in half
oil for deep frying

To make the syrup put the sugar, water and cardamom pods into a pan and heat gently until the sugar has dissolved. Increase the heat and boil for 10 minutes or until the syrup thickens slightly. Pour ⅓ of the syrup into a serving dish and flavour with the rose water.

Sieve the ground almonds, milk powder, semolina, flour and baking powder into a bowl. Heat the ghee or butter and when it is foaming, pour over the dry ingredients in the bowl and mix well until the fat is evenly distributed.

Gradually work in enough beaten egg to give a stiff, but pliable, paste. Knead lightly and form into approximately 24 smooth balls. Press half an almond into the centre of each, then roll into fat sausage shapes.

Slowly deep fry the jamuns in 2 or 3 batches, turning them occasionally. When they are light brown in colour and have fried for 4-5 minutes, drain and place in the hot syrup. Continue in this fashion until all the jamuns have been cooked and soaked. When the syrup is cold and the sweets are impregnated with syrup lift them into the reserved syrup and chill until required.

Sweet Cheese Ladoos

Ladoos are made of very many different ingredients but are always shaped into balls. They are usually eaten as a daytime snack or are given as gifts to guests. These are a fairly soft variety, others are crunchy.

140 g (5 oz) ghee or butter
140 g (5 oz) fine semolina
140 g (5 oz) caster sugar
1 teaspoon caraway seeds
140 g (5 oz) heavy curd cheese
2 tablespoons desiccated coconut

Melt the butter in a heavy-based pan and stir in the semolina. Cook as gently as possible for 25 minutes, stirring all the time and making sure that the semolina does not brown. Mix in the sugar and caraway seeds off the heat and let the mixture cool completely.

When it is cold work in the curd cheese and shape into smooth bite-sized balls. Put the desiccated coconut onto a plate and roll the balls in it to give a nice coating. Chill the ladoos for at least 2 hours to allow them to harden slightly.

Index